Ma(

VIKTOR SCHRECKENGOST

Designs In Dinnerware

Jo Cunningham

Schiffer Publishing Ltd

4880 Lower Valley Road, Atglen, PA 19310 USA

Back cover: Portrait of Viktor Schreckengost courtesy of Herb Ascherman.

Designed by "Sue"
Type set in Americana XBd BT/Zurich BT

ISBN: 0-7643-2522-1
Printed in China
1 2 3 4

Published by Schiffer Publishing Ltd.
4880 Lower Valley Road
Atglen, PA 19310
Phone: (610) 593-1777; Fax: (610) 593-2002
E-mail: Info@schifferbooks.com

For the largest selection of fine reference books on this and related subjects, please visit our web site at
www.schifferbooks.com
We are always looking for people to write books on new and related subjects. If you have an idea for a book please contact us at the above address.

This book may be purchased from the publisher.
Include $3.95 for shipping.
Please try your bookstore first.
You may write for a free catalog.

In Europe, Schiffer books are distributed by
Bushwood Books
6 Marksbury Ave.
Kew Gardens
Surrey TW9 4JF England
Phone: 44 (0) 20 8392-8585; Fax: 44 (0) 20 8392-9876
E-mail: info@bushwoodbooks.co.uk
Website: www.bushwoodbooks.co.uk
Free postage in the U.K., Europe; air mail at cost.

Dedication

This book is dedicated to the memory of two very special people in my life,
Ann Kerr and Don Schreckengost.

Ann was the dearest friend of my lifetime. She was my mentor, my encourager, and my confidante. Ann was not only a grand lady; she was also this country's leading authority on Russel Wright and his work. Ann passed away in September 2001.

Don was an extremely talented artist who was always willing to share his vast and remarkable knowledge of the American pottery industry with anyone seeking that information. My special friend, "Schreck," passed away on December 24, 2001. I will always miss his friendship, the phone calls, the visits, and his wonderful stories (which he always preceded by saying, "This is very interesting," and it always was!)

My life has been truly blessed by these two special friends, and I will always miss Ann and "Schreck." My heart will never be the same.

Author's Note

I have only scratched the surface of Viktor Schreckengost's dinnerware designs. There is much yet to be learned. I have compiled lists of the decorations on dinnerware designed by him, and perhaps more information will be forthcoming. Again, I thank the staff of the Viktor Schreckengost Foundation, Viktor and Gene Schreckengost and Charles Nowacek, Director of the Foundation, for their wonderful support and help. This book would not have been possible without that help.

I also hope that readers will send me information and pictures of pieces that I did not have available for this book. Eventually, it is my desire to complete the Viktor Schreckengost dinnerware design information. You are invited to write me at 535 East Normal, Springfield, Missouri 65807 or email me at mamadish@aol.com with any additional information concerning Viktor Schreckengost dinnerware designs.

Acknowledgments

I am deeply honored to have been invited to participate in the Viktor Schreckengost National Centennial Exhibition in 2006. The dinnerware segment is a small, but important, part of Mr. Schreckengost's vast design output over the years. This book could not have been possible without the help and support of the Viktor Schreckengost Foundation. Not only were the Schreckengost archives available for my use, the Foundation provided many of the images in the book from the Viktor Schreckengost archives.

My thanks and appreciation go to the Foundation staff for their generous cooperation and support, especially: Heather Carr, Archival Assistant; Derrill Dalby, Photographer; Sunny Morton, Public Relations; Craig Bara, Archivist; and John Ely, Graphic Designer.

A very special "thank you" goes to Chip and Lee Nowacek and family, Katie, Hailey, and CJ. Also, and most importantly, to Gene and Viktor Schreckengost, for their most gracious and kind hospitality during my stay. Thanks to all of you for a memorable visit.

David Stratton and the Salem Historical Society have been wonderful sources of information and help. Many former Salem workers have, tirelessly, answered innumerable questions for me. (Little do they know that there are always more questions on the way!) Thanks to David Shivers, who photographed the Salem pictures from the Salem Historical Society, and to my friend, Pat Wilde, for fielding questions about different shapes, decorations, and time frames. Other former Salem workers helped identify shapes and decorations.

A special thanks goes to Katherine Lottman, Margery Strabala, Barbara Wright, Sally Sweeny, Mr. and Mrs. Richard D. Miller, Tammy Quinn, Paul Gresh, Sr., Camille Franzen, Tiffany Knight, Kathy Remish, Dixie Gordon, Al Linder, and Dorothy Hinchliffe. Some of these folks are former Salem workers, and others loaned items to be photographed. I am grateful to Doug Brandt, to Dery Zeppernick, and to Susan Jevens of American Girl, who each sent photographs and information. Thanks also go to my friend, Pat Preuss, for helping me out when I was overwhelmed; to Kathy Audet, for loaning a picture at the last moment; and to my friends at our local Osco Drug store, Kent Miller and Tina Walling, who always made a special effort to process my photographs and achieve the best results.

Elizabeth Gulacsy, Art Librarian and Archivist, Scholes Library, NYS College of Ceramics at Alfred University, Alfred, New York, sent me the information about Alfred Unversity, and I am grateful.

I would be remiss to leave out my good friend, Darlene Nossaman, who always helps me figure out the many dinnerware puzzles and listens to my frustrations. Thanks, Darlene.

And last, but certainly not least, "thanks" is not a big enough word to cover the support given to me, over the years, by my very special friends and helpers *extraordinaire,* Michael Rechel and Ralph Palmieri. I hope you both know how much I treasure our friendship.

Contents

The American Dinnerware Industry

The American dinnerware industry has been a serious interest of mine for more than thirty years. Still, my favorite quote—attributed to the author Michael Crichton—is, "I still do not know what I still do not know." I am beginning to realize, finally, that there are many things about the pottery and dinnerware industry that I will never know. No one in my family has ever worked in the industry, nor have I, so a first-hand working knowledge is not possible. However, for the past thirty years, I have interviewed potters, workers, designers, and pottery owners, and pored over reams of files, trade publications, advertising, and anything else that would add to my knowledge of the American dinnerware manufacturing process. Therefore, it seems that a little background information would be of interest to collectors and students of the American dinnerware industry.

A young man named James Bennett came to the United States from England in 1834 to find work. After working in the Jersey City, New Jersey, potteries for a couple of years, he set about the country to find a good place to establish a pottery of his own. He found the perfect site on a farm in East Liverpool, Ohio. By 1840, Bennett's first pottery was in business, selling yellow ware down the river. He sent for his brothers and, before long, many English potters came to the East Liverpool area to seek work in the new potteries or to build their own. The East Liverpool area soon became known as the "pottery center of the United States."

These English potters brought with them their own methods of potting, including the shapes, the decorations, and the methods of sizing and selling. Some of these methods were used in the American potteries for years; some things—such as trade sizes—were not changed until the 1950s. The ware that emerged from the kilns of these new potteries was yellow ware due to the local clays that were being used. After a few years, the potters realized that if their potteries were to stay in business, they needed to develop a whiteware.

The city fathers of East Liverpool offered two young men, Homer and Shakespeare Laughlin, a $5,000 bonus to start a pottery for the sole purpose of making whiteware. They accepted the offer, started work on their pottery in 1873, and drew the first whiteware from the kilns in October of 1874. The new whiteware had its share of flaws, but Homer Laughlin was determined to overcome these problems, and became one of the major American dinnerware producers (Homer Laughlin China Company is still in business in Newell, West Virginia). This whiteware was not true china, but an earthenware called semi-porcelain or semi-vitreous. Various potteries improved on this earthenware throughout the years. The term "dinnerware" seems to be a more appropriate and general term for this type of ware.

Consumers in this country considered American-made dinnerware to be inferior to English ware, and many of the early backstamps were designed to make the ware appear to have been English-made. An early Sears catalog even stated, in their advertising, that English ware was superior to American-made ware. About 1875, the potter's association decided, as a group, that it was time to change the backstamps and declare their ware to be American-made. Homer Laughlin led the way with an Eagle-over-Lion backstamp that proclaimed victory over the English wares. Laughlin began using this mark circa 1876-1877, and continued to use it until about 1902.

By the late 1870s, several independent decorating shops had opened in East Liverpool. By 1897, according to a trade paper, "The demand for decorated ware is phenomenal. There are no stocks of plain whiteware in the white granite factories. Everything has been decorated up." The ware was taken from the pottery to the individual decorating shops stacked in horse-drawn carts; obviously, there was considerable loss from breakage! Prior to this time, there were no schools in this country for clay workers; in April 1896, Professor Orton started the first such school at Ohio State University and The New York College of Ceramics at Alfred University was established in 1900. The first director was Charles Fergus Binns. One of the first known pottery in-house art directors was a gentleman named Arthur Mountford, a portrait painter who was hired by Homer Laughlin about 1904.

There were no further significant changes in the methods the potters used until the late 1920s and early 1930s.

The Importance of Dinnerware Shapes

Identifying shapes is the most important task that faces the collector. The shapes *are* the main thing. There were two annual shows for the dinnerware manufacturers. The largest, and most important, show was in Pittsburgh in January (in July, a smaller show was held).Whoever was responsible for the new shapes worked many months to present a new shape at the Pittsburgh dinnerware show. The easiest, and most economical, way for a pottery to present a new, fresh look was to design a new shape (or redesign an existing shape) of hollowware to combine with an existing flatware shape. Once the new shape was designed and named, the decorative possibilities were endless. The line could be presented undecorated; decorated with gold or platinum bands or lines, or colored-glaze bands or lines; decorated with decalcomanias alone; or given decals with the different bands or lines as additional decoration. The ware could also be decorated in different-colored glazes on the newly designed shape. These methods of decorating made it possible to maximize the use of one shape of ware. Potteries did everything possible to cut costs and to make use of materials that were on hand.

Early 1900s American dinnerware shapes. Most of the early shapes were standard shapes used by all of the American potteries. This is a catalog page, from 1916, for the Homer Laughlin China Company, East Liverpool, Ohio.

Designers

By the late 1920s and early 1930s, changes in the development of shapes and treatments of the ware began to appear at the potteries. In 1927, Frederick Rhead, a studio potter, became art director at the Homer Laughlin China Company, and Joseph Palin Thorley and Gale Turnbull were hired to design for the American Chinaware Corporation (a short-lived company that was only in business from 1929 to 1931). In the 1930s and 1940s, names such as Russel Wright, Eva Zeisel, Walter Dorwin Teague, Sascha Brastoff, J. Palin Thorley, Gale Turnbull, Vincent Broomhall, Rockwell Kent, and Don and Viktor Schreckengost began to play very important rôles in the dinnerware industry in this country. By the mid- to late 1940s, designers had become a necessity to a pottery. Harrison Keller, President of the Salem China Company, in a speech given before the Design Division Program of the American Ceramic Society Convention (April 23, 1956 in New York City), said of Viktor Schreckengost,

"A good designer is one of the most important single jobs in a plant. It is just about as all-encompassing as that of general management. He must thoroughly understand the plant—the limitations and abilities of the workmen—the limitations of the machines—the market to be covered and the necessity of designing a product that will be instantly accepted—easy to make—one with no losses—and one that will be priced within that market, yet show a top profit. Stated that simply, and in so few words, makes it sound easy—one that may not be totally interesting—possibly due to lack of sufficient challenge. I can assure you that is not the case—such a job is really 'big time poker.' The success or failure of a plant depends on the selling of its output.

Viktor Schreckengost—since the late 30s—has served most capably as our design director. He is chiefly responsible for the development of our Salem 'product' and 'design thinking.' I feel sure much of his early work proved a decided stimulus and forerunner to the 'art', as a whole, and specifically, to those that have more recently become associated with the dinnerware industry.

Keller ended his talk with, "Finally, the use of capable and experienced designers in product development is no longer a *luxury*—it is a necessity in today's manufacturing effort."

Talent—A Schreckengost Family Affair

Adda and Warren Schreckengost had moved from Kittaning, Pennsylvania, to Sebring, Ohio, to find work in the new potteries built by the Sebring family. The Schreckengost family was a multi-talented family, with music and art playing an important role in the family's activities. Pearl was the first of six children born to Adda and Warren. She was the piano player of the family. Ruth was the second child, and had a talent for decorating and crafts. The third child, Viktor, played a musical instrument and displayed his talent for drawing early in life; then Paul, Don, and Lucile. When the parents went out, the Schreckengost children were given drawing projects. The selected winner of the evening was taken for an ice cream treat. The boys also made small toys and marbles from clay, and their father fired the pieces at the pottery. Mrs. Schreckengost made marble bags from flour sacks for the boys.

Paul Gruber Schreckengost

Paul Schreckengost was born January 1, 1908. He graduated from Sebring (Ohio) High School and attended the Cleveland School of Art (now the Cleveland Institute of Art). In 1929, he began working for the Gem Clay Forming Company in Sebring, where he stayed in the position of chief design engineer until retiring in 1976.

During the 1930s and 1940s, Gem Clay designed and produced a wide range of ceramic products, mostly decorative items, including lamps, planters, TV lights, and kitchen products. Paul is credited with designing the black panther lamps that were so popular in the 1950s. During World War Two, he designed and engineered some of the first efficient fireplace logs, radiants, furnace liners, and many other ultrahigh-temperature products.

Paul was, most of all, a family man. He and his wife, Betty, raised eight children and turned down job opportunities that would have furthered his career but would have required moving the family. They stayed in Sebring, where Paul put a small ceramic studio in his basement. He continued to work, nights and weekends, at home, designing and making molds for Salem China, Grindley, Stanford, and many others. These designs included a line of products for Corning Ware, sports figures for Stanford, and the first decorative tile for Summitville (before Don took the head designer position). Brothers Vik and Don often commented that he (Paul) was the most versatile designer, and best mold maker, with whom they had ever worked. His designs are sought after not only by serious collectors, but also by major museums. The teapot shown was auctioned at Sotheby's in December 2005 and sold for $33,000. [Information contributed by Paul Schreckengost's son.]

Ultra-modern teapot designed by Paul Schreckengost. The teapot was sold at a Sotheby's auction in December of 2005, for $33,000.

Tom and Jerry bowl, cups, and ladle. No price established

Don Schreckengost

Don was the next Schreckengost son to study at the Cleveland School of Art. While still at the Cleveland School, Don was in a musical group called "Don, Tom, and Don, The Masters of Rhythm." The group was on their way to a job in Chicago when Don received a telegram, saying, "Job waiting at Salem China if you report immediately." His life's work was chosen at that moment. He took the job at Salem, and one of his first shapes was "Tricorne". Don was invited to teach at Alfred University and, in 1935, he accepted the position. He was made a full professor in 1939. Don became Director of Design at the Homer Laughlin China Company in 1945, and created many award-winning shapes and designs in the 15 years he was employed at Homer Laughlin. Don did freelance design work after leaving the Homer Laughlin China Company, dividing his time between the Hall China Company and the Summitville Tile Company. Don Schreckengost passed away December 24, 2001.

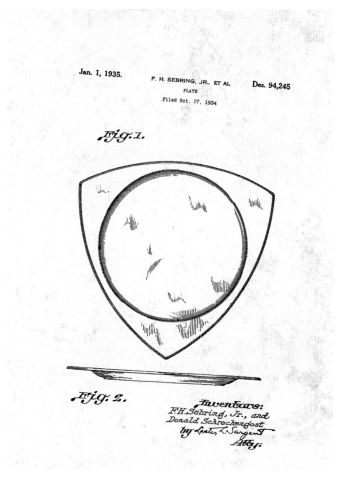

Patent for Tricorne shape held by F.H. Sebring, Jr. and Donald Schreckengost, filed October 17, 1934

Tricorne backstamp patent #94245

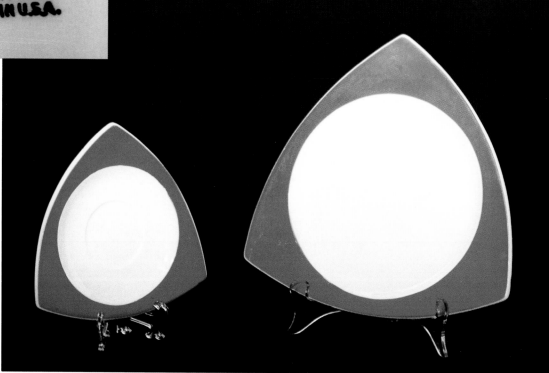

Mandarin Red Tricorne saucer and plate, made by the Salem China Company and designed by Don Schreckengost.

Don Richard Eckelberry

Don Eckelberry was born in Sebring, Ohio, in 1921. From his earliest recollections, he drew whatever interested him at the time. While he was still a youngster, he received an air rifle as a present and began to shoot birds with it. Curious about the birds he shot, Don saved his money and bought bird books to identify the birds. His Uncle, Viktor, gave him a pair of binoculars so that he could watch birds instead of shooting them. By the age of 13, Don Eckelberry had formed a bird club, was writing nature columns for two newspapers, and had his very own one-man art show. Following in the footsteps of his uncles, he, too, studied at the Cleveland Institute of Art. After Cleveland, he went to California and Florida to study birds.

Cardinal on Salem coupe shape plate also by Don Eckelberry $25-30

Bluejay decoration on Salem coupe shape plate from a drawing by Don Eckelberry, $25-30

A friend, John H. Baker, asked Mr. Eckelberry to join the staff of the National Audubon Society, a position he took for a period of time. He began to travel and paint birds, and was eventually asked to illustrate an *Audubon Bird Guide.* He left the Audubon staff so that he could freelance. He gained national recognition after illustrating about 1250 birds found in North America and the north of Mexico. Don Eckelberry died in January 2001.
[From "A Tribute to Don Schreckengost," August 31, 2002 Dedication, Sebring McKinley High School and B.L. Miller Elementary Murals.]

Viktor Schreckengost— Meet the Master of Design

The Master of Design – Viktor Schreckengost

Viktor Schreckengost was born June 26, 1906, in Sebring. He attended school in Sebring and graduated from the Sebring McKinley High School where he played tennis and the saxophone and, as the story goes, spent a lot of time drawing in the margin of his textbooks. While he was still in high school, the French China Company used one of his early drawings. The resulting decal was used later by the Salem China Company on several different shapes and was called "Colonial Fireside". Also while he was still in high school, Viktor's father suffered an accidental fall at the pottery and was disabled for a year or more. With his father's pottery working days ended, Viktor was forced to become the breadwinner for the family. He went to work at the Gem Clay Forming Company, a company in Sebring that made clay mantle rings for stoves. Viktor also did freelance work for other potteries in Sebring.

After high school, Mr. Schreckengost attended the Cleveland School of Art. An exhibit he visited after graduation prompted his desire to study under Michael Powolny at the Kunstgewer-beschule in Vienna, Austria. In order to finance the trip to Vienna for an interview, Viktor both earned a traveling scholarship and also borrowed money. He was accepted as a student and worked with both Professor Powolny and Joseph Hoffman, who critiqued his work.

While Viktor was in Vienna, Guy Cowan contacted him with the offer of a job, which the young man could not refuse. It was for Viktor to work part-time at the Cleveland School of Art and part-time at the Cowan Pottery. Around 1930, he returned to Cleveland and became a designer for the Cowan Pottery as an assistant to his former teacher and mentor, Guy Cowan.

During the time he worked at Cowan Pottery, Viktor designed a restaurant line for the Onondaga Pottery in Syracuse, New York. This line was called "EconoRim" and it proved to be so popular that Onondaga (later, Syracuse China) produced it for more than 70 years. The narrow rim on "EconoRim" line allowed a larger well that held more food in a smaller space, and the ware also stacked well for storage. Thus, it was ideally suited to the needs of hospitals, institutions, railroad dining cars, and steam ships.

Also while at Cowan, and when he was just 26 years old, he designed his most famous and well-known piece, the *Jazz Bowl.*

The famous Jazz Bowl

The Jazz Bowl

The *Jazz Bowl* is easily Viktor's most famous work, as well as an icon of the Art Deco era. Featured at the traveling *Art Deco International Exhibition 2003-2005*, the bowl exudes the modern sensibility and glamour of urban nightlife during the height of Prohibition in the United States. Collectors regularly pay six figures for a *Jazz Bowl* (one sold at Sotheby's in December 2004 for $254,400), but there's more to *Jazz* than a single punch bowl design. Schreckengost created at least ten *Jazz*-related pieces, a stunning series of variations on the "bowl called *Jazz*."

Viktor created the first *Jazz Bowl* in 1930 at the request of First Lady-hopeful, Eleanor Roosevelt. As a part-time potter at Cowan Pottery in Rocky River, Ohio, Viktor was assigned (without being told the client's name) to create a punch bowl with a "New York-ish" theme. Viktor later recalled, "I thought about it awhile, and felt that the City of New York reflected the excitement and energy of jazz music. I listened to a lot of it when I had visited the city. I also felt that the bowl should be blue to mirror the strange, blue-tinged light that rose over the city at night. I started with plaster, creating a bowl, and then went to white porcelain, and started to use a rather primitive method of scratching (etching) an image on the surface of the bowl. This was a black-and-white technique. I then put on the bowl translucent copper and cobalt blue glazes that were then baked on."[1] He gave the punch bowl a parabolic shape, so that the eye extends straight upward past the rim, as if in tribute to the skyscrapers engraved on the side of the bowl. The images celebrate a night on the town: Times Square, The Cotton Club, Radio City Music Hall, a cocktail party. Stars, high-rise building, streetlights, and signs fill the remaining space, which is colored by a brilliant Egyptian-blue glaze over black engobe.

"A week after the bowl was shipped, the gallery called to say that the lady who ordered it was so pleased that she wanted to order two more," continued Viktor. "She said that her husband, Franklin, loved it, too. One was to be sent to her home in Hyde Park, New York, and the other to the White House in Washington. The lady was, of course, Eleanor Roosevelt."[2] Roosevelt's gallery, Brownell-Lambertson, placed its own order for fifty more bowls. Such a positive response led Viktor to produce at least ten *Jazz*-themed punch bowls and decorative wall plaques, some of which were put into production and some of which were one-of-a-kind pieces created for exhibitions.

[The article was contributed by Sunny Morton, Public Relations director for the Viktor Schreckengost Foundation.]

1. Mark Favermann, "Viktor Schreckengost: An American Design Giant," *The Journal of Antiques and Collectibles* (January 2001), pp 27-29.
2. Ibid.

From the *Jazz Bowl* to Dinnerware

Viktor set up a studio in Sebring, Ohio, around 1932. There, he thought about, and designed, dinnerware designs that could be mass-produced. One of his first such independent designs features what can best be described as concentric circles cut into the clay; this became "Peasant Ware", Viktor's first known dinnerware shape. Examples of "Peasant Ware" were included in a dining room that was designed by Donald Deskey for an exhibit at the Metropolitan Museum of Art.

During the early years of the Depression, when production had fallen by one-third at the Limoges China Company in Sebring, the company knew that something had to be done if the pottery was to survive. Frank Sebring's grandson, Donald Albright (who was in charge of the Limoges China Co.), contacted Schreckengost about designing new dinnerware shapes for them, and Viktor offered his "Peasant Ware" line. The management felt it was too modern and not a suitable shape for their customers' needs at that time. (The Limoges China Company, like other potteries in the area, was still deeply entrenched in adaptations of traditional European shapes and decorations). Nevertheless, Viktor accepted the challenge but had little time to design two new shapes for the January 1933 show. It was, by this time, October 1932, and too late to order decals or plan decorations. Viktor made sample lines that could be decorated with bands of color by the decorators at the American Limoges plant.

Apparently, the Limoges management saw the potential in the young Viktor's designs and, in 1933, hired him as their designer. His first shape for the Limoges Company was "Americana"; another shape, "Diana", was introduced in 1934.

New Designer for Limoges

Viktor Schreckengost, well known ceramic artist, has joined the staff of the Limoges China Co., Sebring, Ohio, in charge of design. Since joining Limoges, Mr. Schreckengost has patterned two new shapes which will be shown at the Pittsburgh Show for the first time. This brilliant artist has also developed many novel and attractive decorations in keeping with the lines of the new shapes.

Since graduating from the Cleveland School of Art in 1929, Mr. Schreckengost has earned a considerable reputation as a pottery designer. Born in Sebring and of a long line of pottery makers and designers, he has served as instructor in design at the Cleveland School of Art and as assistant to R. Guy Cowan at the Cowan Pottery Studios.

In the same year that saw his graduation from the art school, he began his studies under the well known professor, Michael Powolny, in Vienna, Austria. Besides having his work shown in a number of exhibitions in Europe, it has been exhibited in the Metropolitan Museum of Art, New York City, American Contemporary Ceramic Show at W.J.Sloane Galleries, New York, and at the exhibition of the New York Ceramic society at the Brownell Lambertson Galleries, New York. A complete gallery was given his work at the Akron Art Institute; a one man show at the Eastman-Bolton Gallery, Cleveland, and a piece of sculpture,"Jeddu-Congo Woman," was shown at the Art Institute of Chicago. He has exhibited in the Pennsylvania Museum of Fine Arts, Philadelphia, and many other places.

He is permanently represented in the Cleveland Museum of Art, where at the annual exhibition of Cleveland Artists and Craftsmen he was awarded first prize in 1931 and in the same show in 1932 he received a special prize for outstanding excellence.

In 1931 he was commissioned to design a pottery punch bowl for Mrs. Franklin D. Roosevelt. He called it "The New Yorker," using a pattern of skyscrapers and music notes. The result was an order for fifty additional from the concern, which had negotiated the commission for Mrs. Roosevelt.

Mr. Schreckengost spent several months in 1932 visiting the pottery centers of Europe—Berlin, Dresden, Prague, Vienna and Paris—as well as other places in Spain, Algeria, France, and Spanish Morocco. During his trip in 1939, he spent considerable time in Russia, Poland, and Hungary.

[Reprinted from December, 1933 issue of *Crockery and Glass Journal*.]

Working Together

Not only were the three Schreckengost brothers extremely talented, but at times they shared each other's workloads. Should one of them have an abundance of work to complete, another of the brothers would pitch in and help. Paul Schreckengost's son recalls his father working in the basement on designs, to help Don. Viktor recalls giving his younger brother, Don, designs to help Don to get started in the business. Don helped Viktor by drawing some of the trademarks. They truly enjoyed sharing and helping each other.

While commendable, this wonderful tendency of helping one another has made the sorting out of

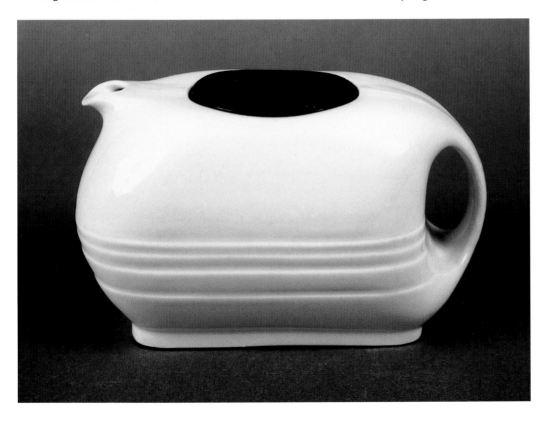

Refrigerator bowl and cover made at Gem Clay Products, Sebring, Ohio. It is not clear which brother designed this particular piece.

shapes and decorations difficult and even, at times, impossible. The shapes of a dinnerware line are the most important part of dinnerware history. Registered patents generally protect dinnerware shapes for a period of time. Even though the patent owners' names can be identified, patent records do not help to unravel the Schreckengost brothers' shared contributions.

It seems reasonably accurate to assume that Viktor Schreckengost designed the shapes presented in this book. Some of the decorations also have been proven to be his designs. There are, however, some decorations that we have not been able to conclusively attribute. The decorations that appeared on *known* Viktor Schreckengost shapes are brought together for the first time in this book. When information has proven, positively, that the decoration can be attributed to Viktor Schreckengost, it is so noted. It appears that sometimes designers felt there was no point in copyrighting decorations. As Viktor Schreckengost explained to the author, "the slightest change in the decoration, a change in the color of a leaf or any small change, could make the design available for someone else's use." He also related that once the designer and company were finished with a decoration, and they released that design, it was then available for anyone to use.

The Viktor Schreckengost National Centennial Exhibition

More than one hundred simultaneous shows—the world's largest exhibition—opened around the country in the hundred days leading up to Viktor Schreckengost's 100th birthday on June 26, 2006. The Viktor Schreckengost National Exhibition series, unprecedented in scope and size, was the only setting large enough for a centennial tribute to one whose influence has been so pervasive. Organized by The Viktor Schreckengost National Centennial Celebration, these exhibitions of Viktor's art and design works opened between March 18 and June 26, 2006, and many remained on display as part of their hosts' permanent collections.

The exhibition content and the venues themselves evidenced the diversity and scope of Viktor's work. From multiple branches of the Smithsonian Institution to local historical societies, universities to restaurants, libraries to public schools, the range of venues and their audiences showed the broad appeal of Viktor's design and artwork. But the variety of works shown was just as stunning: his work was shown in pedal car museums that specialize in theater arts; military art collections; a restaurant with

one of the largest collections of Cowan Pottery; ceramics and decorative arts museums; and more.

Dinnerware enthusiasts were able to see Viktor's dinnerware at multiple locations around the country. Four such locations were the Kirkland Museum in Denver, Colorado, and two historical societies in Ohio's "pottery belt." The Kirkland Museum, according to its website, "has a nationally important display of 20th century decorative arts, with more than 3000 works on view of Arts & Crafts, Art Nouveau, Wiener Werkstätte, DeStijl, Bauhaus, Art Deco, Modern, and Pop Art." The Kirkland owns a *Jazz Bowl*, a set of Viktor's Freeform Primitive dishes, and some greeting card plates. Two additional venues include the Sebring Historical Society and Salem Historical Society, both in Ohio. Sebring is Viktor's hometown and Salem is the home of Viktor's employer, Salem China; both have large collections of Viktor's dinnerware.

Finally, American Girl, the company that sells the famous doll series of the same name, participated as well. The American Girl doll named Molly has a miniature tea set that is a replica of Viktor Schreckengost's 1935 American Limoges design, "Flower Shop" (also sold under the name "Posey Shop"). According to Viktor, "Flower Shop" was immensely popular: twenty-eight railroad cars full of the dinnerware design sold at Higbee's [department store] alone, when the pattern hit the stores. Thirty imitations of the pattern appeared within a year. American Girl displayed original pieces of "Flower Shop" at multiple locations around the country.

For additional information about the exhibition series, and to find out where Viktor's works may be seen, visit www.viktorschreckengost.org.
[Contributed by Sunny McClellan Morton, Public Relations Chief for the Viktor Schreckengost Foundation.]

American Girl Molly and the Flower Shop china doll set

American Limoges China Company: A Family Affair

The Sebring Dynasty

Piecing together the histories of most American pottery companies is a daunting task, at best, because secondary sources provide conflicting information and many primary sources are lost or are unavailable. The job becomes infinitely more complicated whenever the Sebring family is involved, at the very least because the Sebrings seem to have been both a prolific and insatiably entrepreneurial bunch. The Sebring family enterprises included innumerable—and frequently inter-related—companies that amount to a "who's who" of 20th century American potteries. Firms such as Crescent China, E.H. Sebring China, French China, French-Saxon China, Leigh Potters, Limoges China, Oliver China, Royal China, Salem China, Saxon China, Sebring Pottery, and the Strong Manufacturing Co., are just some of the companies that were

founded, owned, and/or operated, variously, by Charles, Ellsworth H., Frank A., Frank H., Frederick (Fred), George A., George E., Joseph, and Oliver H., to name but a few of those industrious Sebrings.

Fortunately, the histories of the two companies under consideration here are relatively straightforward, with F.A. Sebring serving as the connecting link between them.

By most accounts, Frank A. (F.A.) Sebring established the Sterling China Company adjacent to the Sebring Pottery Company, in 1900. For whatever reason, the company name soon was changed to the Sebring China Company. (According to Floyd W. McKee, the resulting confusion of the company names required representatives from each company to appear at the Sebring post office to examine incoming mail in order to determine to which company the mail belonged!)

The (American) Limoges China Company, Sebring, Ohio

It seems that, by July 1904, the company name was changed again, to The Limoges China Company, under which name it operated until 1949. In that year, Haviland et Cie., in an alliance between French porcelain makers and the City of Limoges, France, threatened to sue The Limoges China Company, concerning the use of the Limoges name. This group maintained that only china made from French Limoges-area clays should be able to use the "Limoges" name. Accordingly, The Limoges China Co. (of Ohio) changed its name, officially, to The American Limoges China Company. According to Harvey Duke, the Ohio company had been using "American Limoges" in its advertisements since the mid-1930s.

Initially, the company manufactured "real" china (that is, thin porcelain products, such as dinnerware, tea sets, and chocolate, salad, fruit, and soup sets) under the direction of a skilled expert from Central Europe. The company seems to have converted to using semi-vitreous ware about the same time it assumed the name Limoges China Company. According to one source, this changeover was affected after a disastrous fire occurred during the company's third year of business. The fire destroyed most of the equipment and all of the company's records and formulas, and resulted in the death of the European ceramist.

Frederick (Fred) Sebring managed the firm from the time it was rebuilt (circa 1904) until 1911, when he started The Saxon China Company. By 1918, Frank A. Sebring's son-in-law, W.I. Gahris, was managing Limoges. Frank "Tode" Sebring, Jr., was serving as the company's Secretary, a position he left, in 1919, to become President and General Manager of the Salem China Co.

J. Harrison Keller joined the management team at American Limoges in 1936. In a curious turn of events, W.I. Gahris's daughter, Gretchen [who was, therefore, F.A. Sebring's granddaughter], eventually married J. Harrison Keller, who became president of Salem China Company in 1950. The American Limoges Company ceased operating in 1955.

The American Limoges China Company reportedly had a daily production of 45,000 pieces in about 1950. Aside from producing immense quantities of semi-vitreous dinnerware, the quality of which equaled its numerous competitors, American Limoges' "claims to fame" include the first use of the tunnel kiln, the introduction of decalcomania for decorating, and the development of the first "industrial ceramic laboratories." Viktor Schreckengost began designing for the American Limoges company in 1933, developing some of its most successful dinnerware lines, including "Americana" (1934), "Diana" (1934), "Manhattan" (1935), "Triumph" (1937), and "Jiffy Ware" (1937).

American Limoges Shapes and Decorations

Circa mid-1930s "Peasant Ware"

The first pieces of the Peasant Ware line were hand-thrown by Viktor Schreckengost. He later adjusted the jigger to make ridges in the ware, making Peasant Ware appear to be thrown, even though it was machine-made. Mr. Schreckengost presented his Peasant Ware to the Limoges China Company about 1932, but they determined it was too modern for their buyers. Peasant Ware was never mass-produced; only a few sample items were made. No prices for the Peasant Ware have been established.

Peasant ware tumblers. Because Peasant Ware was not mass-produced, no prices are established for Peasant Ware.

Stunning black Peasant Ware with Gold trim.

Black Peasant Ware bowl.

Peasant Ware creamy yellow bowl set with tan and brown trim.

Peasant Ware bowl, plate, cup, saucer,
creamer, sugar bowl with cover, teapot.

Peasant Ware, creamy yellow with tan and
brown trim. Sugar and cover, dinner plate,
salad plate, cup/saucer set, teapot, creamer.

Peasant Ware bowl with shades
of Salmon and tan trim.

1934 "Americana" Shape

The Americana shape and the Diana shape (p.22), both Viktor Schreckengost designs, were introduced in 1934 by the (American) Limoges China Company Company. The Americana shape was said to be one of the first mass produced "modern dinnerware" shapes. The Americana shape was a huge success. In January 1934, Frederick Rhead, in *Chats on Pottery*, said of the new shapes, "these two shapes constitute the most outstanding creative development by any American pottery within the last year". This was quite a compliment coming from Frederick Rhead, an artist in his own right.

Some of the decorations found on the Americana shape are Smoke, Flame, and Oleander. Some of the decorations on all of the shapes may not have been produced.

Americana shape from a June, 1934 *Crockery and Glass Journal*.

Americana Shape, "Ultra" decoration plate. $18-20.

1935 "Diana" Shape

The Diana and Americana shapes were both well received. These two new shapes not only brought Limoges capacity production up, they exceeded their capabilities and found it necessary to rent space from other potteries to keep up with the demand for the new shapes. Diana has a slightly fluted shape.

Early decorations found on the Diana shape are Evening Star, Joan of Arc, and Comet.

"Polka Dots" on the Diana shape. Mazarine Blue dots with blue line trim. Left to right, sugar and cover $25-30, dinner plate $14-16, Jug and cover $45-55, cup/saucer $15-18 set.

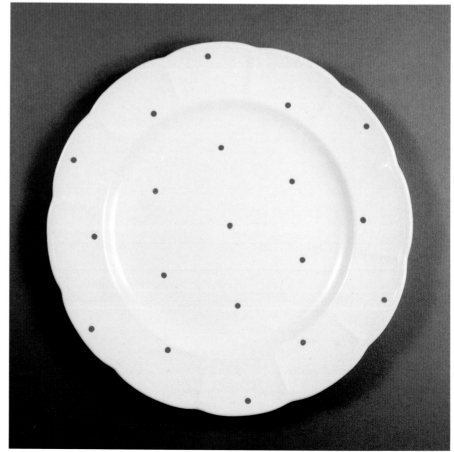

"Red Polka Dot" Diana shape plate $14-16

Not shown, "Joan of Arc" Stamped Fleur-de-Lis decoration on Diana shape.

"The Wren" decoration on Diana plate $14-16

"Dutch Style Flowers" decoration on Diana shape plate $14-16

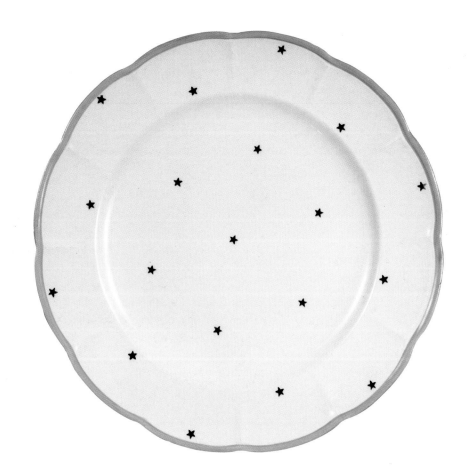

Green Evening Star with
green edge trim $14-16

"Evening Star" with black edge trim
on Diana shape plate $14-16

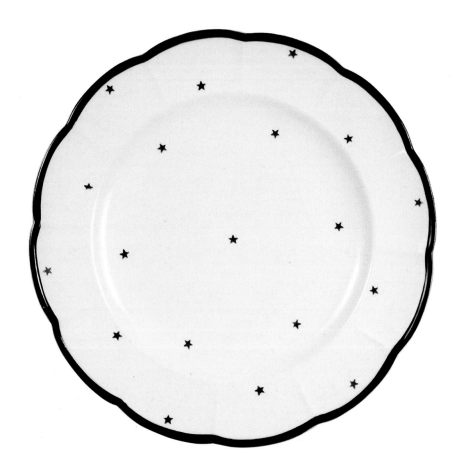

24

1935 "Manhattan" Shape

Decorations found on the Manhattan shape are Flower Shop, Santa Fe, Animal Kingdom, Red Sails, Garden of Eden, and many banded decorations.

Flower Shop on Manhattan shape

1936, Viktor Schreckengost presenting Miss Kate Smith with a Manhattan shape plate with the Harvest decoration.

"Silver Elegance" on Manhattan shape

Meerschaum solid pumpkin colored glaze with brown band and darker brown lines as accent. No price established

Ship Ahoy, a decoration on the Manhattan shape, red line trim decoration. The different flags mean "Good Luck," if you know how to read the flags. Left to right: sugar and cover $35-40, tab handle plate, $10-45, plate $25-30, creamer $35-40, cup and saucer set $20-25, covered dish $55-60

"Birds in a Bush," brown center decoration with three narrow brown bands

The Animal Kingdom decoration on the Manhattan shape is a very intriguing decoration. Red animals on a stark white background with a red line trim. The Animal Kingdom is made up of a mule, elephant, goat, cow, rooster, fish and a squirrel. Do not be surprised to find other animals. Each animal is a "star". A small red star can be found near each animal. Cups each, $25-30 ea, tab handle plate, $18-20

The teapot is part of the Manhattan Animal Kingdom set and is not part of the child's feeding set. The teapot is marked, Manhattan, American Limoges, Sebring-Ohio, Animal Kingdom with the "three skyscraper" mark.
Manhattan Animal Kingdom teapot, $65-75. Each piece of the child's feeding set is marked only Noah's Ark with no other information. *From the collection of Doug Brandt.*
Left to right, 6 ¼" plate $30-35, mug 3" tall $35-45, bowl $35-40.

Red Sails decoration on Manhattan shape plate with narrow red band trim, $18-20

Metropolis – a striking decoration on a Manhattan shape plate with narrow red band trim, $18-20

"Garden of Eden" decoration on Manhattan shape plate with narrow blue line trim, $18-20

Village of the Sea decoration on Manhattan shape plate, $18-20

Chartreuse plate with three shades of green narrow trim. The center decoration also is found on the later Triumph shape, $18-20

"Daphne" decoration on Manhattan. The center decoration is found on other Manhattan and Triumph shapes. Covered casserole $45-55, plate $18-20, cup/saucer set $18-20, creamer $18-20, sugar and cover $25-28

1935 "Snowflake" Shape

This beautiful shape is embossed with snow-flakes and was made undecorated and also with decoration in the center section.

"Winter Blues" decoration on a Snowflake shape plate, $15-18

"Flowers"on a Snowflake shape plate, light red edge trim. $15-18

"Fall Flowers" decoration on a Snowflake shape plate, $15-18

31

1937 "Triumph" Shape

The Triumph shape was introduced in 1937, the same year that the Victory shape was introduced by the Salem China Company. The Triumph shape, a reworking of the Manhattan shape, had a band of circular rings or ridges around the outer edge of the flatware. This design was a means of saving money for the pottery, necessary at all times for the potteries, and especially in the 1930s. This new shape provided a less expensive means of decorating the ware. The outer edge of the ware could be painted with wide or narrow bands. Decals were also added in colors that complemented the bands or lines. The Triumpn shape proved to be a very successful shape for the American Limoges Company, and can be found with a variety of colorful decorations.

Triumph Shape from Chicago newspaper ad circa 1937 for Carson Pirie Scott & Company. Top left Oslo, described as "a multicolored Floral Cluster". Upper right: Fiord "A Delightful Stylized Design". Both Fiord and Oslo decorations were available in different colored pastel bands.

June 1939, *Better Homes & Gardens* magazine cover

Chicago Retail Volume Nears 1929 Peak In Holiday Sales

Retail sales in windy city break ten-year records for Christmas volume.

According to reports from Chicago stores, china and glass volume this year came the nearest to approaching the 1929 volume in the past decade. Good general buying throughout December, as well as many particularly heavy days, reduced stocks of dinnerware and stemware as well as fancy china and table glassware which are always well toward the top of the best sellers.
MANDEL BROTHERS – A

CROCKERY AND GLASS JOURNAL for January, 1940

strong half-page Sunday Tribune a on a two-day sale of china and glas more than doubled their day, an sales through the day and evenin reached a peak in this highly suc cessful Christmas season.

CARSON PIRIE SCOTT & CO —In order to make this Decembe one of the best in years, Carson kept their department constantly be fore the public through ads, window and first floor displays. Most lavish use of advertising was a full page i color in the Sunday Tribune fo "Oslo" and "Fiord" patterns in 20 piece sets at $2.95, and open stoc items priced individually. Item from glassware or china section als appeared in each of the several ad headed, "Carson's Gift Guide for th Home." The collection of Fostori was featured as the "most complet in Chicago." Advertised items wer given the best kind of support b department displays large enough t attract the attention of everyon entering the department.

In the manner of past center ais display arrangements, twelve table featured Christmas gift suggestion for mother, father, grandmothe grandfather, sister, brother, bachelo uncle, maiden aunt, boy friend, gi friend, husband and wife. Merchan dise was taken from the gift, chin and glass sections.

ATTRACTIVELY EXECUTED

"STOCKHOLM" pattern on Triumph shape designed for American Limoges China Company by Viktor Schreckengost. Pattern is in Gunmetal and Dubonnet on soft Ivory body, with Salmon color reeded rim.

Stockholm decoration on Triumph shape ad from late 1930s pottery, Glass and Brass Salesman.

Tan Triumph plate, darker tan lines and edge, $16 18

Salmon and grey plate with dark green on Triumph shape, $16-18

Left:
"Green Band" with gold lines on Triumph shape. Many of the Triumph shapes have colored bands and lines.

"Two Birds in a Bush" with copper trim on Triumph shape, $16-18

Yellow & Tan band on the Triumph shape plate, $16-18

"Teal Flowers" on Triumph shape, $16-18

Pastel Blue and Pink bands on the Triumph shape, plate $16-18

"Paradise Apple" on Triumph shape, $16-18

Bermuda decoration on tan back ground, bright orange bands, $16-18

"Ravine" on Triumph shape plate, $16-18

Jamaica decoration on Triumph shape, $18-20

Greta Dustitone decoration on Triumph shape, $16-18

"Sweet Briar" decoration on Triumph shape, $16-18

"Green Dustitone" decoration on Triumph shape, $16-18

Vanity Fair decoration on Triumph shape, $16-18

Hiawatha decoration with green and yellow lines, $16-18

Pineapple decoration on Triumph shape, $16-18

Empire decoration on Triumph shape with grey and black line trim, $16-18

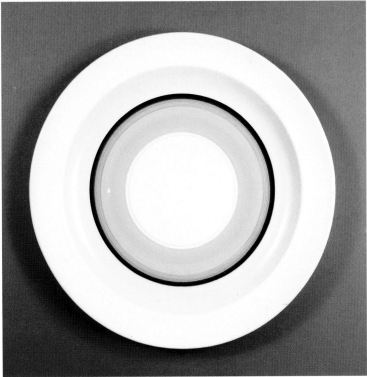

Eclipse decoration on Triumph shape, $16-18

"Dutch Style Flowers" decoration on Triumph shape, $16-18

Zuyder Zee decoration on Triumph shape, $16-18

"Small Flowers" decoration on Triumph shape, $16-18

Twinkle Twinkle on Triumph shape, $16-18

Santa Fe on Triumph shape, $16-18

"Fantasy Leaves" on Triumph shape, $16-18

Gallery on Triumph shape, $16-18

Golden Lace on Triumph shape, $16-18

Green "Two Birds" on Triumph shape, $16-18

Grey with Blue Bands, Blue, Grey bands with gold lines

Grey background with orange trim on shoulder

Blue, green bands on Triumph shape

Bands of oranges and greens with gold lines

"Stylized Leaves" Red, orange, grey leaves, yellow, green, red lines

Harvest on grey background with shades of tan and green

King Charles decoration on Triumph shape, plate $12-14

Rosalie decoration on Triumph, cake plate $15-20, sugar $10-12, creamer $14-16

Antique Car Specialty plates, Oldsmobile Runabout, 1903.
$20-25 each

Antique Car First Packard Automobile, 1899

Antique Car Duryea's Motor Wagon, 1895

Antique Car Selden's Motor Wagon, 1877

Antique Car Ford's First Car, 1896

Antique Car Winton Steubenville, 1898

Antique Car Cadillac Automobile, 1903

Antique Car Autocar Runabout, 1902

"Mermaid" on Triumph Shape plate, $20-25

1937 "Jiffy" Kitchenware

A 1930s trade journal advertisement for "Jiffy" ware relates:

'Jiffy' ware, designed by Viktor Schreckengost for cooking, storing, and serving, was introduced in the Sebring-Limoges showrooms. This ware is modeled along stream lines for convenience in use—the jugs are flattened at the sides, so that several can be stored side by side in the refrigerator; the flat covers can be used also as ash trays or coasters; the covered grease pot is 'splashless'; the handled salt and pepper shakers 'shake' from the side rather than the top. Made in ivory, with wide, flat handles and bands in red, green, blue or yellow—also decorated with decals.

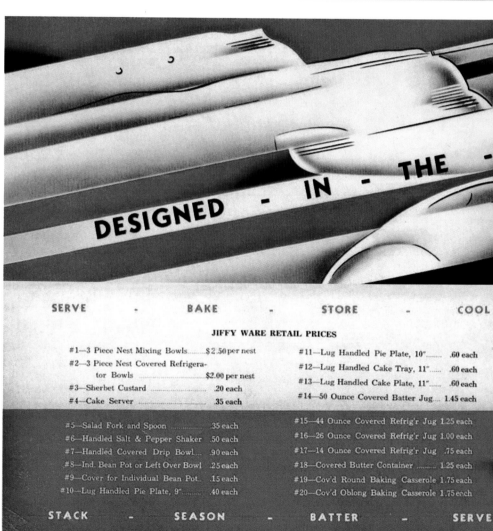

Jiffy Kitchenware brochure

DESIGNED - IN - THE -

SERVE - BAKE - STORE - COOL

JIFFY WARE RETAIL PRICES

#1—3 Piece Nest Mixing Bowls $2.50 per nest	#11—Lug Handled Pie Plate, 10" .60 each
#2—3 Piece Nest Covered Refrigerator Bowls $2.00 per nest	#12—Lug Handled Cake Tray, 11" .60 each
#3—Sherbet Custard .20 each	#13—Lug Handled Cake Plate, 11" .60 each
#4—Cake Server .35 each	#14—50 Ounce Covered Batter Jug 1.45 each
#5—Salad Fork and Spoon .35 each	#15—44 Ounce Covered Refrig'r Jug 1.25 each
#6—Handled Salt & Pepper Shaker .50 each	#16—26 Ounce Covered Refrig'r Jug 1.00 each
#7—Handled Covered Drip Bowl .90 each	#17—14 Ounce Covered Refrig'r Jug .75 each
#8—Ind. Bean Pot or Left Over Bowl .25 each	#18—Covered Butter Container 1.25 each
#9—Cover for Individual Bean Pot .15 each	#19—Cov'd Round Baking Casserole 1.75 each
#10—Lug Handled Pie Plate, 9" .40 each	#20—Cov'd Oblong Baking Casserole 1.75 each

STACK - SEASON - BATTER - SERVE

46

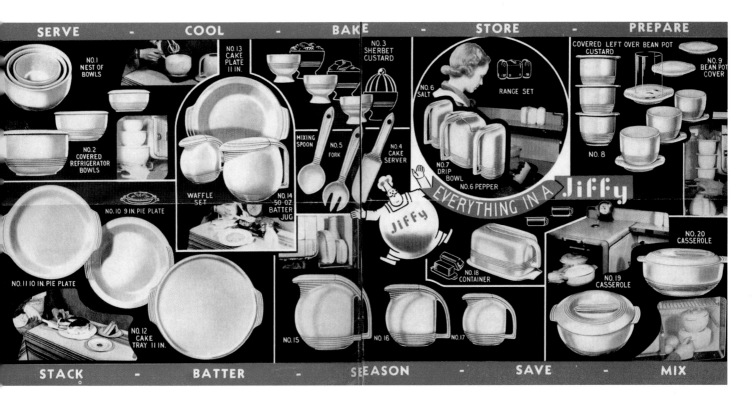

Jiffy Ware and Triumph display at Atlantic City Dupont Exhibit in May, 1938

Covered Casserole $60-65

Red and White Jiffy Ware, left to right: #2 covered refrigerator set, bottom $50-60, middle bowl $40-45, small bowl $30-35, Front Casserole $60-65, leftover bean pot and cover $40-45

Yellow Jiffyware – not produced, no price established

Deep Chocolate Brown Jiffyware – not produced, Left to right – Refrigerator jug, small #17 in brochure, lid to jug, covered bowls, medium #16 jug, salt and pepper set. No price established

1940 "Candlelight" Shape

The Candlelight shape is a more formal shape than Schreckengost's previous designs.

Candle Light is the name of this new dinnerware shape from Sebring Pottery Co., simple and graceful in line. The Abundance pattern which adorns it is done in muted tones.

Abundance decoration on the Candlelight shape

"White Oaks" by

AMERICA LIMOGE

"Traditionally "Old South" in spirit. Reminiscent of crin dresses, jasmine blossoms and white columned verandas. American in feeling—Modern American in style and adaptabil

White Oaks decoration on Candlelight shape

Commonwealth decoration on Candlelight shape, from 1941 Crockery and Glass Journal. A Della Robia style of decoration

FOR

Enduring Memories

AT THE DINNER TABLE

In its *National Bouquet*, Limoges achieves a new note for American dinnerware. Here Viktor Schreckengost, recognized as leader among ceramic artists, gathers together all our State Flowers. His composite is a superb design in brilliant natural colors. Truly American, *National Bouquet* offers vivid opportunities for All-American settings.

If seeking a more conventional motif, you'll like Della Robbia with its warm colors and renaissance motif. You'll find these and many others, *open stock* . . . economically priced, at better stores. Or if you'd like to have descriptive leaflets, just write to Department 542.

Top Left, National Bouquet decoration, a composite of all the state flowers. To the right, Della Robbia. Both decorations on American Limoges Candlelight shape. The advertisement is from a 1940s magazine.

AMERICAN LIMOGES

★ ★ ★ ★ ★ ★ ★

Look for the name American Limoges ...handmade by American craftsmen

REPLACEMENT OR A REFUND OF MONEY
Guaranteed by Good Housekeeping
IF DEFECTIVE OR NOT AS ADVERTISED THEREIN

With this Seal—your additional buying protection

THE LIMOGES CHINA CO., SEBRING, OHIO

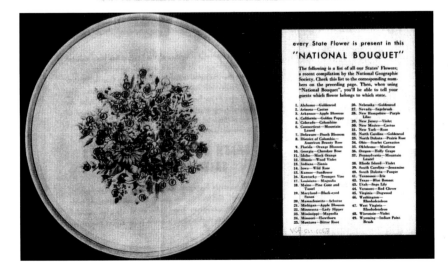

National Bouquet decoration on Candlelight shape

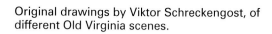
Original drawings by Viktor Schreckengost, of different Old Virginia scenes.

The Old Virginia decoration on the Candlelight shape, both in blue and maroon, depicts scenes from Williamsburg, Virginia, early 1940s

OLD VIRGINIA
by Limoges

Superb Design . . . and a name you'll be proud of

In the early 1940s, everything was patriotic in America. The patriotic theme was not only in dinnerware, but in all home furnishings. Viktor Schreckengost eloquently wrote the following article in the early 1940s, which remains in the company archives (document VSFsn9591). He signed the article, "Viktor Schreckengost, Art Director and Designer for American Limoges China Co., Sebring Pottery Co, Salem China Co."

The American Theme in Dinnerware

We have all become so much more American-conscious, at least we start to realize what the home of the free really means. The American Theme has become such an important influence in every field— music, theater, dress, home and home furnishings. If dinnerware is to fit into or take its place in this scheme, what can we do?

It is said that a Style is the interpretation of Art of a Certain Time. Will this be a Style or just a passing fad?

As we look at the Life of America we find Three great Styles. Each has its own character and personality, each reflects a stage in American history, but they all have the same basic elements of Design.

The first, of course, is Colonial. How can we interpret the spirit of this time in the present scheme? In practically every other branch of home furnishings we find fine old examples from which to work. However, we find no American dinnerware of this period. We must look at old Staffordshire from England or at ware from the Orient. It is true, they were made for the American trade. Stars, stripes, eagles and all the other motifs appear. It is not enough to take any shape in production and put on it, a picture of an early American home, a piece of embroidery, a quilt or a fashionable lady of the day. One must start with the Shape. No greater inspiration culd be found than the fine old silver by such master craftsmen as Paul Revere or Jacob Hurd. If we can but capture the spirit and feeling, proportions and forms and adapt them to our material, means of production and way of living, we have come closer to the American Theme.

For Decoration, no richer or more abundant field could be found than the second of these Styles, Federal. It has been recognized by Designers in practically [every] phase of furnishing the home. Allthough much too ornate for most people of our time, it is lavish and bountiful in ideas. From the elaborate geometric patterns and the profusion of floral clusters, deep heavy, luxurious colors and wealth of gold, there are new softer and more restrained trends emerging.

America has been known as the "melting pot". This is especially true of the third Style, American Modern. It is the fusing or blending of the Swedish, French, English, German, Austrian and all other Moderns. It is the New Style which reflects the Art of out times. Look to Colonial for the spirit and feeling, the Federal for richness and maturity, adapt them to our Modern American way of life and you Have the real American Trend. Of Americans, by Americans and for Americans.

Viktor Schreckengost also coordinated the Federal theme for Carson Pirie Scott about the same time, for their Wishmaker line.

Attracting customer attention at the point-of-sale is the fastest route to increased volume . . . greater profits. And this new Limoges Display was designed to attract the attention of your customers

Daphne decoration on Candlelight shape. From an early 1940s advertisement

Federal Coral Pink

THE YEAR'S MOST OUTSTANDING DINNERWARE ACHIEVEMENT

Here is the Key to your problem of increased sales.

Year after year Limoges favors its customers with "Smart" New patterns which establish a precedent in the dinnerware field.

Customers acceptance of our ware has reached new heights in our experience.

The accelerating enthusiasm shown by so many buyers should be interesting to you.

THIS IS ONE OF OUR BEST SELLING NUMBERS

Write for a Limoges catalogue of the year's twelve best selling patterns. These 12 patterns are all carried in stock for your convenience.

THE AMERICAN LIMOGES CHINA COMPANY

Sebring, Ohio

Federal Coral Pink on the Candlelight shape. Also made in Federal Araby Blue. Early 1940s advertisement. Other colors may have been available.

1940 "Embassy" Shape

The Embassy shape was a redesign of an existing Limoges shape. No photograph was available. Embassy was not one of Mr. Schreckengost's more successful shapes.

Salem China Company

Early picture of the Salem China Company

Officers of the Company

A group of officials associated with The Standard Pottery Company, of East Liverpool, Ohio, grew disenchanted with the future prospects for potteries in East Liverpool and looked for a location at which to develop a new plant, in 1898. They were attracted by the offer of a "modest bonus" (elsewhere recorded as $ 22,500 plus some land) that was tendered by residents of Salem, Ohio. The group, including Patrick and John McNicol, E.J. and William ("Biddam") Smith, and Daniel P. and Cornelius Cronin, contracted to build a five-kiln plant at the proffered site in Salem. The new company was incorporated, later in 1898, as the Salem China Company. Construction began in January of 1899 and, by June, the plant was fully operational except for the decorating department, which was scheduled to open by November of that year.

T.J. McNicol was the founding President and William Smith served as Secretary, Treasurer, and General Manager. In 1913, McNicol and Smith sold their shares in the company to local businessmen, leaving D.P. Cronin as President. For some little while, the company apparently suffered from an unfortunate combination of absentee management and under-capitalization.

Through machinations that are far from clear, Patrick McNichol contrived to sell the company, in the summer of 1918, to F.A. Sebring, in order for Sebring to provide a future for his son, Frank "Tode" Sebring, Jr. Then, F.A. Sebring invited Floyd W. McKee to run the company until "Tode" could assume control. In 1919, "Tode" left his position with the Limoges China Co. to become President and General Manager of Salem China Co. Thus, by August of 1918, the Salem China Co. came into the Sebring family realm.

After "Tode"'s untimely death, in December of 1934, his father, F.A. Sebring, assumed the presidency of Salem China Co, while Floyd McKee served as Vice-president and General Manager. Upon F.A. Sebring's death, in 1937, McKee became President and General Manager of Salem China Co., a position he held until he retired, in 1950, and became the Chairman of the Board.

Next, J. Harrison Keller, formerly with American Limoges Co., became the President of Salem China Co. Production at Salem ceased in 1967; but the company continued to operate during 1968 and afterward as a "sales and service organization," (otherwise known as a distributor).

Production

Salem China Co. initially produced "white granite" ware, and, later, semi-vitreous dinnerware and kitchenware, eventually becoming "an outstanding maker of fine dinnerware." By the time the company reached its 50th anniversary in 1949, it was producing more than 15 million pieces per year. Noteworthy shapes that were produced by Salem include "Briar Rose" (1932), "Heirloom", "New Yorker" (1933), "Streamline" (1933/34), "Trend", "Tricorne" (1934), "Century" (1935), and "Bonjour" (1936).

Viktor Schreckengost began designing for the company in the mid-1930s and, in 1946, he was named chief designer. Among his most successful shape designs are "Victory" (1937) "Hotco" (1937), "Symphony" (1940), "Tempo" (1948), "Contour", "Lotus Bud" (1950), "Flair" (1951) briefly referred to as "Fortune", "Ranch", "Ranchstyle" (1951), "Constellation" (1953), and "Free-form" (1955).

1937 "Victory" Shape

At the Limoges China Company, Viktor Schreckengost's Triumph shape was selling well. In 1937, he was asked by the Sebring management to help with designs at their Salem China Company. They wanted to provide Salem with a shape that was along the same lines, yet different, from the circular ridges in the Triumph shape.

Viktor Schreckengost's answer for Salem was the Victory shape. On the Victory shape, the narrow ridges go up and down, as opposed to the circular rings on the Triumph shape. Victory seemed to be immediately accepted and the name was perfect for the time. Many decorations and treatments were used on the Victory shape.

The first decoration shown at a trade show is derived from the *Godey Prints* book from the late 1800s. We know positively this decoration was not a Viktor Schreckengost design. J. Palin Thorley, a designer for the American China Corporation, redesigned a decoration from the original Godey print. While Godey prints were used by many potteries and were popular at the time, they were not designed or redesigned by Viktor Schreckengost.

The Victory shape was described at the time: "The perfect lines and perfect symmetry that characterizes this handsome set make it unusually smart and popular. The border deviates from the standard floral embossing by being fluted. The handles on the hollow pieces are convenient and attractive. This pattern has a stateliness hard to surpass." Many different decorations and treatments were used on the ever-popular Victory shape.

The first decoration shown on the Victory shape is a Godey Print from the Godey Book of Prints from the late 1800s.

Godey Print from a Salem sales promotion, top left Imperial shape (not designed by Viktor Schreckengost). The Imperial shape was used for the service and specialty plates.

Victory shape, Petit Point Basket or Basket of Flowers decoration, plate $12-14, also used on the Salem's earlier Century shape.

VIENNA DESIGN

A very beautiful pattern, with rose center design, and rose lace border effect. A lovely blue and ivory background helps to bring out the attractive colors in this design. The beauty is further enhanced by the wide ivory band, which encircles the verge of this ware bordered with brown lines on each side. This makes a very pretty effect, and shows up to marvelous advantage on the snow-white body of the new Victory dinnerware, which is of the very latest style and design.

Vienna decoration on Victory shape from late thirties wholesale catalog.

The undecorated Victory shape was called Victory.

The graceful lines and perfect symmetry that characterizes this handsome set make it unusually smart and popular. The border deviates from the standard floral embossing by being fluted. The handles on the hollow pieces are convenient and attractive. Although undecorated, this pattern has a stateliness hard to surpass.

Possibly part of the "Cadet Series." Lines form the only decoration on this series. Several different colors were used to decorate the Cadet Series. Temporary Name, "Cadet One."

Golden Pheasant

GARDEN DESIGN

A beautiful bouquet of flowers, with red and yellow tulips predominating adorn the center of this ware. A coral line on the verge surrounded by a heavier grey band which harmonizes with the background of the center design, giving a final touch to this attractive decoration. The handles are especially treated in grey and coral. The shape is the new "Victory" designed by a famous ceramic artist of the Cleveland Art School. It represents the last word in ceramic designing.

Garden Design, red and yellow tulips decorate this Victory shape.

A SMART, MODERN SHAPE SET OFF BY ATTRACTIVE DESIGNING

Bright gay flowers feature this decoration, with yellows and greens predominating. Dainty orchid buds also enhance the attractiveness of this lovely design. It is a two spray design. The handles are treated in appropriate colors.

This "Jane Adams" pattern is as attractive as a refreshing summer floral spray. It sets off the modern dining table to such great advantage that knowing hostesses are unusually enthusiastic about it. You, too, can be sure that what it does for other tables it most assuredly can do for yours. The new "Victory" shape forms a perfect background for the smartness of its modern pattern. You will be interested in knowing that this shape was designed by a noted ceramic designer of the Cleveland Art School. This is truly a lovely shape.

Jane Adams on Victory shape.

Tulip decoration on Victory shape.

This "Doily Petit Point" pattern on the new Victory shape is an outstanding contribution to modern designing. This very beautiful pattern embodies all the dignity and grace of rare old lace. The design features a beautiful rose center with a floral border, all worked out in the new Petit Point or cross-stitch design. The handles are all treated with a wide gold bar giving added attractiveness to this decoration. A fawn background adds the final touch to this lovely pattern.

The shape is the new "Victory," designed by a noted ceramic designer of the Cleveland Art School. Surely if you are interested in fine furnishings for that home of yours this beautifully shaped chinaware so smartly decorated will appeal to you. You will find listed below three different size sets, one to meet the requirements of any size family.

Doily Petit Point on Victory shape.

Striking New Decorations

The Salem China Co.
SALEM, OHIO

Parkway decoration on Victory shape.

Parkway decoration on Victory shape shakers.

IParkway decoration on Victory shape plate, $12-14

Striking New Decorations

The Salem China Co.
SALEM, OHIO

Sun Valley decoration on Victory shape.

Cruiser decoration, appears to be the same as Cadet Series, Cruiser many have been a specific color decoration. From 1937 *Crockery and Glass Journal*

Dominion decoration on Victory shape.

Bountiful decoration on Victory shape.

Blue Basket decoration on Victory shape.

Top left: Doily Petit Point, right: Indian Tree, Middle Row: Tulip, Avon, Bottom Row: Rose Bowl, Red Sails.

Indian Tree Victory plate $12-14

Advertisement for free Victory dinnerware with coupons.

INDIAN TREE

Originally created by the celebrated English designer, Thomas Minton, in the 18th Century, this design has been popular ever since. This pattern gives you a combination of a beautiful legend, plus a lovely decoration. This pattern is rich in gay flowers, featuring deep pinks, blues, and yellows supported by colorful foliage. It has real eye-appeal and is meeting with splendid acceptance on the part of discriminating buyers.

Colonial Fireside advertisement from May 1947.

1937 ad for Corona decoration on Victory shape.

1938 ad from *Crockery and Glass Journal*. "Bright shoulder treatment on the Victory shape at Salem China Company is offered in green, yellow, maroon, lipstick, red and periwinkle blue. The sugar and creamer are in solid colors."

DECORATION No. 60171 S. H.

leverly designed informal decoration created /ictor Schrechengost. Five conventionalized t subjects done in lovely tones of green, yel-, rose and purple that impart an appearance and painted artistry.

The name "Bountiful" not only typifies the lu beauty of the decoration but expresses the boun ful pleasures derived from the use of this al gether charming dinnerware design. Availal in sets and open stock.

Bountiful, a different fruit on each piece, called the new Fruit Series.

Sante Fe decorations, described as "striking bright colors in decoration decal with bright red line trim."

"Art Deco Vase with Shade," original name not known. "Soft blue narrow band compliments the decoration."

CROCKERY AND GLASS JOURNAL for August, 1937

Original names not available for these decorations on Victory. Temporary names left to right, "Lily Pads," "Leaf Spray," "Circle of Flowers"

Avon on the Victory shape and Lansdowne on Symphony—two new dinnerware patterns from Salem China Co., with the handfilled prints in rich colors.

1937 "Hotco"

The Hotco refrigerator storage line was introduced shortly after the Victory shape was released. Again, Viktor Schreckengost was asked to provide something like American Limoges' Jiffy Ware, yet be different. His answer was the Hotco line for Salem. In the Jiffy line, horizontal lines go around the base of the pieces. On the Hotco refrigerator line, there is a narrow edge of fine ridges (like Victory) that go up and down at the bases of the pieces. Some of the Hotco pieces have the same decorations as the Victory dinnerware.

Hotco blue and white refrigerator jugs. Left to right: $50-55, $45-55, $40-45.

Hotco red and white salt and pepper shakers $25-30 each

Hotco Kitchenware ad from a 1938 *Crockery and Glass Journal*, "can be used for baking, and refrigerator storage, is gracefully streamlined, and may be had in decorations to match dinnerware." Sante Fe decoration.

Hotco refrigerator jug and cover. Petit Point Basket decoration. $40-45

Below:
Hotco refrigerator jar with original label, gold stamping on outside, rose decorations inside.

HOT-CO WARE

For Baking • Storing • Cooling
Serving • Seasoning • Stacking

Hot-Co Ware will stand constant use in oven or refrigerator. For best service, do not subject to sudden changes in temperature. Do not wet cloth in removing from hot oven. With ordinary care, it will last indefinitely.

THE SALEM CHINA CO.
SALEM, OHIO
40 Years of Fine Dinnerware

1940 "Symphony" Shape

When the Symphony shape was introduced in 1940, it was described as follows: "This lovely shape, by Viktor Schreckengost, is different from anything on the market today. Refined, beautiful, charming in its simplicity. Its chaste lines express a new high point in elegance and distinction. Lends itself to a great variety of decorations."

The Symphony shape remained in the Salem line for several years. The shape of the Symphony plates are similar to the American Limoges Candlelight plates.

SALEM CHINA'S SUPERB NEW CREATION FOR 1940

This lovely shape, by Viktor Schreckengost, is different from anything on the market today. Refined, beautiful, charming in its simplicity. Its chaste lines express a new high point in elegance and distinction. Lends itself to a great variety of decorations. See this new shape and other Salem productions at the Pittsburgh Show, January 8 to 16, Suites 507-9, William Penn Hotel.

Viktor Schreckengost, Head of the Department of Design, The Cleveland School of Art. Winner First Prize Ceramic Sculpture for National Ceramic Show. Awarded Charles Fergus Binns Medal for the Highest Achievement in the Field of Ceramic Art in 1938, given by the American Ceramic Society and Alfred University.

THE SALEM CHINA CO. »»»» SALEM, OHIO

CROCKERY AND GLASS JOURNAL for January, 1940

1940s ad showing Salem China's new Symphony shape designed by Viktor Schreckengost.

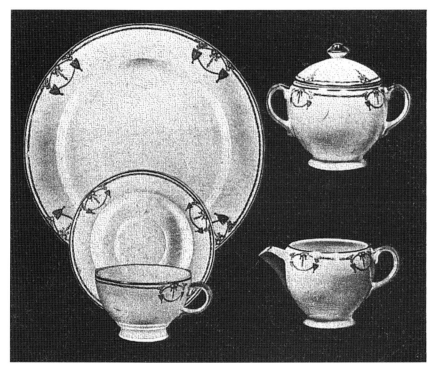

Commodore Pattern

Always in good taste and harmonizes with any table setting. 23K. gold of unusual beauty and appeal. Delicately traced border and classic medallions of gold.

Nation wide acceptance among all types of stores and buyers has proven the continued popularity for this type of pattern. Featured on the plain Symphony Shape with wide rims and creamy white surface, making a perfect background for a pattern of this kind.

Commodore decoration on Symphony shape

Small ad for Bryn Mawr decoration on Symphony

BRYN-MAWR PATTERN

Shapes of New Symphony shape

Platter 15"		Plate 11"
Platter 13"		Plate 10"
Platter 11"	Chop Plate 13"	Coffee Server	Covd. Casserole	Dinner Plate 9"
Platter 7"		Creamer	Plate 8"
Gravy Boat		Covd. Butter	Pie Plate 7"
Gravy Boat (1 pt)			B & B Plate 6"
Chowder	Cake Plate 10"	Covd. Sugar	Oatmeal
Coupe Soup 7"	Deluxe Salt or Pepper Shakers	
Nappie 8"	Baker 9"	Pickle Dish	Gravy Bowl	Cup & Saucer	7" Salad Plate	Fruit Dish	A. D. Cup & Saucer

Antoinette decoration on Symphony shape plate $14-16

Ming Ling decoration on Symphony shape plate $14-16

Garden decoration on Symphony shape plate $14-16

Claudia decoration on Symphony shape plate $14-16

A Salem ad for Claudia decoration on a Symphony shape
plate, $14-16

Orchard decoration on Symphony plate $14-16

Fantasy on Symphony shape plate $14-16

Sheffield on Symphony shape – front plate $14-16, top coffee server $45-50, top right sugar & cover, $20-28, creamer $18-25, cup/saucer set $15-18 set. From Salem sales ad

Ad for Lansdowne decoration on Symphony shape

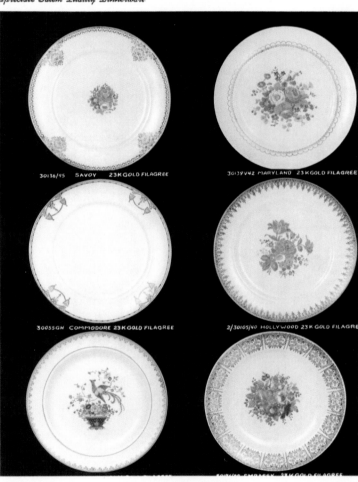

appreciate Salem Quality Dinnerware

30136/95 SAVOY 23K GOLD FILAGREE

30139V42 MARYLAND 23K GOLD FILAGREE

30055GH COMMODORE 23K GOLD FILAGREE

2/30105/40 HOLLYWOOD 23K GOLD FILAGRE

EMBASSY 23 K GOLD FILAGRE

Symphony plates from a Salem advertising. Top row, left to right, Savoy, Maryland decorations. Middle row: Commodore, Hollywood. Bottom row, Golden Pheasant, Embassy

Lansdowne decoration on Symphony shape plate $14-16

30 147/44 COURTSHIP 23 K GOLD FILAGREE

5/ 3008 GEORGIAN SALMON

30874 GE WILTSHIRE

30 140/48 BELVEDERE 23 K GOLD FILAGREE

30 GB148 WESTCHESTER

3050 ETUDE

The Salem China Co.
SALEM, OHIO

Top row, left to right: Courtship, Georgian Salmon, Middle row: Wiltshire, Belvedere. Bottom row: Westchester, Etude

Sensational Success

23 K GOLD FILAGREE

Hawthorne decoration on Symphony shape

74

Build your dinner service at your convenience to fit your needs. These open stock pieces are readily available.

Tea Cups - - $ .45		Oblong Vegetable Dish 9"	.90
Tea Cups & Saucers - .70		Round Vegetable Dish 8"	.90
B & B Plates 6" - - .35		Gravy Bowls 1-pt. -	.60
Pie Plates 7" - - - .40		Gravy Boats 1-pt. .	1.25
Sq. Salad Plates 7" .45		Gravy Boats (F/S) -	2.75
Breakfast Plates 8" .45		Stand attached	
Dinner Plates 9" .55		Pickle Dish - - -	.45
Lg. Dinner Plates 10" .65		Cake Plate 10"	.80
Fruit Saucers - - - .25		Chop Plate 13"	1.35
Oatmeals or Cereals .40		Cream Pitcher - -	.90
Coupe Soups 7" - - .50		Covered Sugar	
Chowders - .50		Bowl -	1.80
Demi-tasse Coffee Cups and Saucers .60		Covered Casserole	3.25
Meat Platters 7" - .55		Salt and Pepper Shakers pr. -	1.35
Meat Platters 11" - .80		Coffee Server	
Meat Platters 13" - 1.35		(8-Cup) -	3.55
Meat Platters 15" - 2.25			

FORM NO. 61E

AS ADVERTISED IN BETTER HOMES & GARDENS

Debutante BY SALEM

A BRIDAL GIFT OF Lasting Loveliness

Advertisement for the Debutante decoration on the Symphony shape.

Debutante decoration on the Symphony shape. Plate $12-14, Victory shape shaker $18-20, Cup saucer set $14-16 set.

1948 "Tempo" Shape

The Tempo shape, introduced in 1948, was described as, "new in both shape and decorations, in modern vein, offered in five new patterns, all decals." It was also offered in Dewtone, "Broad firm lines of gray, salmon, blue or yellow are the sole decorations of the Dewtone series on the Salem China Tempo shape. The marked simplicity of this pattern and the flowing lines of the shape commend it for contemporary table settings."

Parsley was one of the new decorations. "Parsley, in three tones of green, imparts a clean, fresh appearance to Tempo's modern, flowing lines"

Orchard was a new pattern on the Tempo shape. "Here's the pattern to get behind to get ahead. Colorful, attractive and moderately priced."

Viktor Schreckengost inspecting a Tempo shape coffee server.

The Tempo shape introduction ad from a trade paper

Parsley decoration on Tempo shape $14-16

All Parsley decoration on Tempo tea pot, $45-50; casserole
and cover $45-50; creamer $20-25; sugar and cover $25-30

Parsley

Parsley was one of the first decorations used on Tempo

Strawberry Patch decoration on Tempo $14-16

Original black and white advertising photo of Strawberry Patch

Garden Decoration on Symphony plate $14-16

Original black and white advertising photo for Garden

Orchard

While in New York see ORCHARD
...at our salesrooms—1107 Broadway

Here's the pattern to get behind to get ahead. It's colorful, attractive and yet MODERATELY PRICED... within reach of every one of your customers. It's easy to sell Salem Dinnerware because Salem national advertising consistently reaches over 16 million homemakers. So while you're in New York for the June Show, be sure to visit our showrooms. See this and Salem's many other lovely and profitable patterns.

HERE'S THE LINE TO GET BEHIND TO GET AHEAD

SALEM
NATIONAL ADVERTISING
consistently reaches over
16 million homemakers!

THE **S**ALEM CHINA co.

SALEM, OHIO   *Established 1898*

SALES OFFICES: *New York:* H. G. Heckmann, 1107 Broadway, Chelsea 2-8848 • *Chicago:* Williams & Son, 15-125 Merchandise Mart, Superior 8922 • *San Francisco:* Leo D. Holtzberg, 274 Western Merchandise Mart, Un. 1-2727 • *Denver, Portland, Seattle:* The Vinton Co.

Add for Orchard decoration on Tempo shape, 1949, *China, Glass, and Decorative Accessories.*

JUNE 1949 CHINA, GLASS AND DECORATIVE ACCESSORIES

Fantasy decoration on Tempo shape, dated 1950.

Dogwood decoration on Tempo shape

1949 "Lotus Bud" Shape

The Lotus Bud, or Lotus, shape was introduced in 1949, when a news release from the Salem China Company, written by Viktor Schreckengost, read as follows:

Lotus Bud, the new and distinctive dinnerware by the Salem China Company, Salem, Ohio was designed by Viktor Schreckengost to tie in with today's Far East trend in American modern interiors. It is medium priced, semi-porcelain.

Says Mr. Schreckengost, S.I.D. and Dean of the Industrial Design Department, Cleveland School of Art, "Much of what is good in interiors, both from a design standpoint and functional point of view, has come from the Far East. China, Japan, Indo-China, Burma and India have civilizations that are far older and always will be ahead of us in what is basically good, basically functional, and fundamentally lovely. Their art has inherent charm probably because their design, thinking, and creative efforts are the result of thousand of years of effort, trial, and practical use.

This new dinnerware is not a direct acceptance of the Far East. It is based on Far East concepts in design, pattern, and coloring. Adaptations are made, keeping in mind the needs, habits and uses to which American modern dinnerware is put.

Harrison Keller, new head of the Salem China Company, believes that Lotus Bud is more saleable than any shape ever created. He says, "Lotus Bud combines beautifully colored patterns with true simplicity and functionalism of shape never before attained in such a remarkable degree. We are starting with just six different flower patterns but will probably add to these after satisfactory production on the original six is achieved."

A word about the beautiful Lotus shape

Lotus is a new shape, light in weight, created by Viktor Schreckengost in semi-vitreous dinnerware. It is a coupe shape, with a narrow embossed edge, which adds grace, beauty and texture.

distinctive styles hand crafted   since *1898*

Lotus shapes

Ad for the new Lotus shape, from a trade paper

81

Viktor Schreckengost (left) showing Salem management the new Lotus shape.

Antoinette decoration

Antoinette

A pastel bouquet of roses and springtime blossoms encircled by a wide deep green band make this a delightful pattern for any occasion. It will compliment your best silver and crystal.

"Antoinette" is furnished on the light-weight "Lotus" shape, a coupe shape, with embossed rim for added protection and serviceability.

Salem

Antoinette from a Salem sales sheet

Cherry Blossom decoration on Lotus shape. Cherry Blossom coffee Server $60-65, plate $16-18, casserole $50-55

WATER LILY, a new pattern in the modern trend designed by Viktor Schreckengost. Decoration reflects Far Eastern influence now being offered on "Lotus Bud" shape. Scheduled for national advertising program in Fall. Salem China Company, Salem, Ohio.

Water Lily decoration on Lotus shape, ad from trade paper

FARMER IN THE DELL

Farmer in the Dell decoration on the Lotus shape from a Sears 1950s catalog. The Far East line of the Lotus shape was made up of the Water Lily, Moon Flower, Cherry Blossom, Antoinette, and Chrysanthemum and Wisteria. The Godey Prints decoration also was used on the Lotus shape.

83

1951 "Ranchstyle" Shape

From a Salem sales sheet, we learn that:

The Ranchstyle shape, introduced in 1951 was a full coupe shape; described as modern and flowing with gracious hollowware pieces. Each item is designed for maximum utility. Ranchstyle is available in a wide selection of attractive, popular priced decorations.

Many of our retail store special promotions are presented on Ranchstyle because of it's proven popularity and it's ready adaptability to center decorations, side sprays, and even decorated edges.

Among Salem's most popular promotional patterns were:

Whimsey, a delicate center spray of silvery gray flowers with brown leaves and stems; luminous as a cloud.

Meadow, a small center decoration of dainty pink stylized bachelor buttons; understated simplicity.

Tea Rose, a large yellow rose with half-opened bud, with bright shining green leaves.

Vassar Rose, a deep pink moss rose; Victorian rose with half-opened bud, with bright shining green leaves.

Embassy, a dainty dark pink rose center design, timeless — yet ever fresh and new.

Pen and Pencil, a modern abstract design of charcoal and grey pen and pencil scrolls.

Chateau, a conservative pastel nosegay design; delightfully appealing.

Riviera, a buoyant charcoal and turquoise scroll design encircling the inside edge of the plate.

Primrose, a shower of flame-colored blossoms and buds contrasts with leaves of rich green. It's a styling advance to keynote exciting new table settings.

Melody Lane, all the lilting quality it's name implies; brilliant floral bouquet with a hand-painted look.

Westchester, a turquoise stylized flower with charcoal leaves and stems. Subtle elegance in it's simplicity.

The first advertisement known for Ranchstyle was for colored glaze ware, with no decoration. The Ranchstyle shape on the coupe shape (round shapes) was offered "in your choice of four solid colors: Lime Yellow, Pine Green, Birch Gray or Maple Red. Mix-em, match 'em to create your own styling in modern table settings of informal beauty. It's the big seller-a complete line by Salem China…a fifty year tradition of quality, reliability and advanced styling."

The first Ranchstyle decorations on a white background were Melody Lane, Geranium, Talisman, and Primrose. The Ranchstyle was in the Salem line for several years and can be found with many different decorations on the coupe Ranchstyle shape. Apparently Viktor Schreckengost designed only one coupe shape in flatware. The plates were used in many different shapes.

In 1953, Viktor Schreckengost changed the solid colored glazes on the Ranchstyle coupe shape and called it the Sterling Color series. The colors were coral, green, gray, lime, and snow. "The Sterling series had silver-colored bands and handle facings for that extra touch of decorator elegance."

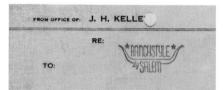

The round coupe shape Ranchstyle colored glaze ware was marked Ranchstyle/Salem. Part of a memo from J.H. Keller giving approval for the new Ranchstyle backstamp designed by Viktor Schreckengost.

Coupe shapes used in Ranchstyle shape

Ranchstyle — a full coupe shape

Designed by Viktor Schreckengost, a modern flowing shape—with gracious hollowware—giving the maximum utility to each item. Available in a wide selection of attractive, popular priced decorations.

1951 Ranchstyle Shape
The Ranchstyle shape used both the round coupe shape and the Flair or "square-round" shape flatware.

distinctive styles hand crafted *since 1898*

by
SALEM
CHINA CO.

Country Gentleman decoration on Ranchstyle plate $14-16

This decoration has been called "18th Century Tulip" plate $14-16. Only a picture of the plate with this decoration was available. Without the holloware it is not possible to know what pattern it belongs to. The 18th Century Tulip is not an official name.

Geranium decoration on round coupe shape plate $12-14

Geranium decoration on the round coupe Ranchstyle shape.

RANCH STYLE

The four colors featured in our Ranch-style line of colored glazes include— A deep rich Pine Green—A delicate Lime Yellow—A soft Birch Gray—A sparkling Cedar Coral.

"Ranchstyle" is furnished on a modern Coupe Shape. All pieces are full size with generous handles giving the maximum utility to each item.

Ranchstyle dinnerware is made by skilled craftsmen. It is fully guaranteed as to quality & workmanship. It is ovenproof & free from crazing.

No color picture available. The Sterling Series was released in 1953 in Sterling Coral, Sterling Gray, Sterling Green, Sterling Lime and Sterling Snow. The Sterling series had "silver colored bands and handle facings for that extra touch of decorator elegance."

the Sterling series

by Salem

Introducing for 1953...Salem's "Sterling Series"... a complete new dinnerware on Salem's popular "Ranch Style" shape. Your choice of five colors in rich solid-tone color-glaze... with silver-colored bands and handle facings for that extra touch of decorator elegance. Write for samples, prices.

STERLING CORAL · STERLING GRAY
STERLING GREEN
STERLING LIME · STERLING SNOW

THE Salem CHINA CO.
SALEM, OHIO
REPRESENTATIVES IN PRINCIPAL CITIES

The first Ranchstyle was introduced in solid glaze colors of Pine Green, Lime Yellow, Birch Gray and Cedar Coral. Ad for Ranchstyle from Salem's sales sheet

Cedar Coral, Birch Gray, Lime Yellow plates $12-14 each

TALISMAN

Warm yellows and foliage greens combine n a rich pattern with a traditional flair. It's table-talk beauty to flatter the proudest hostess . . . compliment the most important occasion.

"Talisman" is furnished on the modern "Ranch Style" coupe shape. All pieces are full size with generous handles giving the maximum utility to each item.

Talisman Rose decoration on the coupe Ranchstyle shape. Ad from Salem's sales sheets for Talisman Rose

Talisman Rose decoration on coupe Ranchstyle shape plate $12-14

Carnation on coupe Ranchstyle shape plate $12-14

Melody Lane brochure

Melody Lane decoration on coupe Ranchstyle shape plate $12-14

Simplicity

Simple in creation, yet delicately intricate and masterfully applied. A lone, sky blue bud appears on a gray-leaved stem. Same motif is repeated five times as the center pattern on the dinnerplates...once on creamer, sugar, cups, saucers, etc. Made on Salem's Ranchstyle shape.

Simplicity decoration on the round coupe Ranchstyle shape

Original watercolor first drawing for the Anniversary decoration used on coupe Ranchstyle shape. There were changes made in the proofing process from the first drawing to the finished decal from the decal company.

TARTAN

From a 1950s Sears catalog.
Tartan decoration on the
coupe Ranchstyle shape

91

Whimsey decoration on the round
coupe Ranchstyle plate

It's Pen and Pencil
on Salem's Ranchstyle
Coupe Shape

Swirling doodles and dots . . . another unusual
pattern by Viktor Schreckengost. Dramatically complemented with black accessory pieces, Pen and Pencil
captures the imagination of contemporary or traditional decor. Available in sets and open stock. A
postcard will bring samples and prices.

Salem THE SALEM CHINA CO.
SALEM, OHIO
REPRESENTATIVES IN PRINCIPAL AMERICAN CITIES

1951 "Flair" Shape

Flair and Ranchstyle shapes were both designed by Viktor Schreckengost in 1951. The shapes were mixed together to make patterns or lines. The Flair shape was a short set, with only 11 different pieces making up the complete shape. The Flair set consisted of three sizes of plates, a platter, a cereal bowl, a serving bowl, a cup and saucer, creamer and sugar (the same as Constellation shape), and another size bowl.

The Flair shape was a combination of the coupe shape and the modern square shape that was referred to as the "rounded square shape. Flair "combines all of the utility of a coupe shape with the charm and uniqueness of the square."

The cup appears to be a coupe shape cup with a slightly different handle. "The angular lines were carried out in the hollowware and accessory items in this shape; right down to square feet on the cups. Flair cups were quite an achievement in production. "The cup has a square outside shape while keeping a round inside shape to combine features of design and ease of drinking."

Maple Leaf decoration on Flair shape platter $18-20

Flair shapes

JACK STRAW ACCENT

A VIKTOR SCHRECKENGOST CREATION

This striking, ultra-modern straw design is in the golden yellow and white on Salem's "Flair" shape. The yellow and white motif of Jack Straw pattern is accented by the brown cups, sugar and creamer.

In the "Flair" shape, Salem has combined all the utility of a coupe shape with the charm and uniqueness of the modern square.

VSFsn9886

Jackstraw Accent on the Flair shape

WOODHUE ON FLAIR

Here it is...Salem's elegant new "Woodhue" pattern...a spray of leaves in forest tones of brown, green and blue, a "natural" for smart modern table settings. On Salem's popular "Flair" shape.

Suggested retail price—
Starter Set, $8.95.

new for '52 by SALEM CHINA

PRIMROSE ON RANCH STYLE

A shower of flame-colored flowers and buds with contrasting green leaves on white...It's Salem's striking new "Primrose" pattern on the favorite "Ranch Style" shape. Suggested retail price—Starter Set, $5.95.

Created by the famous American artist, Viktor Schreckengost, these two new patterns aroused widespread interest at the recent Pittsburgh Show. By Salem China ...over 50 years of styling leadership.

THE **SALEM CHINA** CO.
SALEM, OHIO
Representatives in Principal Cities

Look for this backstamp—the signet of Salem's master potters. It is your assurance of unfailing highest quality.

Woodhue on Flair and Primrose on Ranchstyle round Coupe shape. From a 1953 *China Glass & Decoration Accessories*.

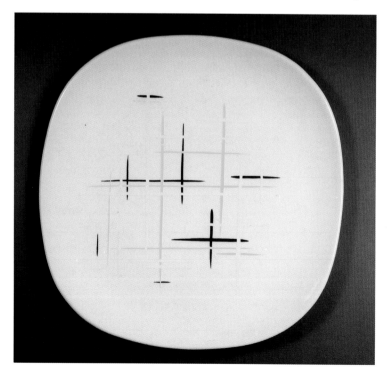

Jackstraw Accent decoration on Flair shape plate $12-14

Woodhue decoration on Flair (?)

94

Fantasy on Flair plate $12-14

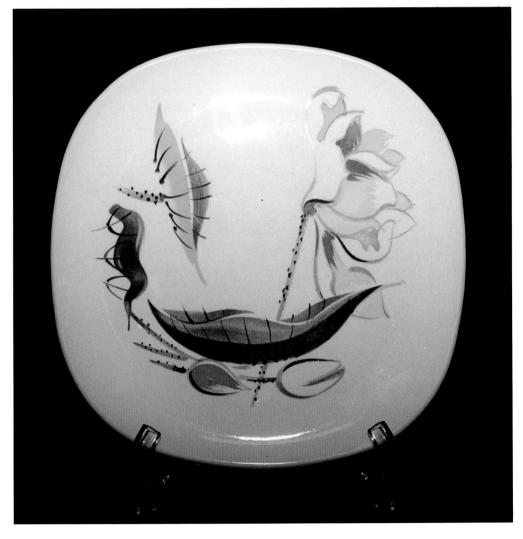

Water Lily decoration on Flair
$12-14

95

Peach and Clover decoration
on Flair plate $12-14

french provincial

by **SALEM CHINA**

wood-tone browns and forest greens
in a pattern of rich tradition

A traditional theme done with contemporary freshness
by Viktor Schreckengost—its rich coloring mellowed by the
Lime Yellow glaze. The shape is Salem's brilliant new
"Flair"...an advanced styling that combines the
coupe shape with the modern square. It's a sales
"natural"—a complete line by Salem China...
over fifty years of styling leadership.

Salem

Look for this backstamp—the
signet of Salem's master potters. It is your assurance of
unfailing highest quality.

THE **SALEM CHINA** CO.
SALEM, OHIO
Representatives in Principal Cities

FRUITWOOD—Same pattern on
modern round "Ranch Style"
shape. Lime Yellow glaze.
AMERICAN PROVINCIAL—Same
pattern on "Ranch Style" shape.
Clear glaze.

French Provincial decoration on
Flair shape from 1950s trade
publication

A French Provincial decoration on the
Lime Yellow glaze Flair shape. This
decoration was called Fruitwood when
used on the round coupe Ranchstyle
shape with Lime Yellow glaze. It was
called American Provincial on the round
coupe Ranchstyle shape with clear glaze.

97

Shaker Brown Lime – Decoration on
Lime Yellow glaze Flair shape

Colored glaze on the Flair shape. Main Street is the name and the backstamp on the Flair colored glaze ware sold by Sears in the mid-fifties. Sears had their own names for the colors in this line. The coral is Jubilee Peach. I have not been able to find names for the other Sears Main Street colors.

The colored glaze Flair shape was also sold to Macy's but may not have been marked. Correspondence between Mr. Schreckengost and the Salem China Company suggested that they might use paper labels for the Macy's ware. No further information was found.

Main Street plates, $12-14 each, saucer $4-6, 7" salad/dessert plate, $6-8

Main Street as pictured in a mid-fifties Sears catalog

1952 Coronet Shape

The Coronet shape met the need for a more formal style of dinnerware.

This is the traditional shape usually associated with fine dinnerware; it's timeless classic beauty is as appealing today as it has been for generations. Always in perfect taste; to serve you proudly on any occasion. Distinctive of this shape are the footed hollowware pieces and the wide rim on the flatware pieces.

Among the patterns shown on the Coronet shape are the First Lady; described as "a dainty center floral arrangement. The rims of the plates, and much of the body of the hollowware pieces are a deep emerald green overlaid with gold filigree; truly a stately pattern."

Blossom Time on Coronet is "a dainty border design of delicate sprays of pale pink apple blossoms. The plates are edged with a fine line of gold.

The leaf decoration has also been called Coronation, with "a dark green wide band and leaves of a lighter green." The Virginian was also used on the Coronet shape, with a gold filigree trim on the shoulder of the wider Coronet pieces. There are more decorations that will show up on this elegant, formal shape. A gold leaf decoration and a wheat decoration were also used on the Coronet shape.

Sepia Fruit on Coronet Shape

Gold Leaf decoration on Coronet teapot $60-70

1952 Christmas Eve Decoration

Christmas Eve is a decoration, not a shape. In a letter to Viktor Schreckengost dated in March of 1952, the Salem China Company's sales manager, J.A. Armstrong, reminded Viktor that Marshall Fields store in Chicago had requested a Christmas Tree decoration to be made for them. Apparently, Salem had a couple of people already working on a Christmas decoration, but management was not pleased with the results. Armstrong asked Viktor to give the decoration some thought, and suggested that if he wanted to submit ideas, that would be even better.

No other correspondence concerning Christmas Eve was found in the archives until a special order, dated December 19, 1952, for Christmas Eve was placed for the Christmas Tree decoration on the "Lime Yellow Ranchstyle Ware – to be done the same as on the white glaze." It seems safe to assume that

Christmas Eve had already been produced on the white glaze.

It is likely that the earliest date for Christmas Eve is 1952. This was another of Viktor Schreckengost's popular designs, found on several Salem shapes. The Christmas Eve decoration was widely copied. Its Christmas tree is very detailed, complete with a train going through a village. Stamped stars in different colors surround the tree and, of course, the initials *"VS"* are found in the lower right corner of the decoration.

Christmas Eve was a popular line for Salem. In 1959, the sales manager for the Salem China Company sent Viktor Schrenkengost the following memo:

Regarding our Christmas Eve pattern, we have apparently had this decal around just about as long as it's gong to be any good to us. Fortunately we do not have too big a stock. We are getting a terrific firing loss on what we are running this year. We had about 1100 sheets the first of September.

While we won't do anything for this year, we should remember that before another season rolls around we will have to do something new; either reorder on the same pattern or come up with a new design. Put this in your file for Salem, and let's discuss.

The Christmas Eve decoration was used on several different Salem shapes over the years. Christmas Eve was a very popular decoration and was one of Viktor Schreckengost's most well-known patterns. The Christmas Eve decoration was phased out in the early 1960s, but when Salem began sending designs overseas to be produced, several of Viktor's Christmas Eve decorations continued to be sold by Salem.

Black and white enlargement of Viktor Schreckengost's Christmas Eve decoration. Notice the "VS" signature on the right base of the tree.

Front center left: 7" coupe shape plate $14-16, left: cup and saucer set, back: a small bowl for dip completes the Dip and Serve set. Plate only $15-20, Coronet shape teapot $50-55, sugar and cover $20-25, creamer $15-20

Cake plate, part of a two piece set, cake server and plate,
plate only $20-25

Christmas Eve plate $20-25

SALEM'S
Christmas Eve

Christmas Eve dinnerware adds that "extra something" to Holiday entertaining.

The items illustrated offer you a well-balanced selection for profitable selling. Order one—or two—or three of the following assortments today.

Index Letter	Quantity	Item	Retail Price Per Item
A	1	Teapot & Warmer	$7.95
B	1	Footed Bon Bon Dish	3.00
C	1	Footed Utility Dish	4.50
D	1	Footed Cake Plate 11"	3.95
E	3	Handled Cookie Trays 10"	2.95
F	8	Tom & Jerry Mugs	1.25
G	1	Tom & Jerry Bowl	6.50
H	8	Square Ash Trays 5½"	1.25
I	12	Round Ash Trays 5"	.60
J	1	Dip 'n Serve Dish	3.95
K	8	Buffet Plates 9" & Cups	2.50
L	2	2 Pc. Cake Sets	3.25
—	8	Cups & Saucers	1.75
—	8	Dinner Plates 10"	1.75

The above assortment retails for $120.40. The dealer's discount is 50%. Terms: Net 30 days, F.O.B. Salem, Ohio.

Check here ☐ for complete price list.

Clip the above list to your letterhead for prompt shipment.

Fine Dinnerware since 1898

Salem CHINA CO.
SALEM, OHIO

Late 1950s, Christmas Eve sales sheet showing different pieces of Christmas Eve on different Salem China shapes.

Not a Viktor Schreckengost design, Noel, also a Christmas tree decoration, was designed by Viktor's brother, Don Schreckengost. Sold by the Salem China Company, Noel was not manufactured at the Salem China Company.

103

1953 Constellation Shape

Constellation shape was described as "a stunning, new pattern designed by Viktor Schreckengost for contemporary homemakers. Round and square shapes combined with a charcoal-gray and off-white color combination make Constellation a standout for formal or informal use." Viktor Schreckengost also designed the wire stand and candleholder for the Constellation shape. Constellation is a mixture of the coupe shape flatware, cup and saucer. Constellation, Flair, and Ranchstyle shapes were all designed about the same time. The shapes were used interchangeably.

News Release, November 15, 1953:

HERE'S THE STORY BEHIND THE DESIGN OF SALEM CHINA'S CONSTELLATION LINE

Almost a quarter century ago Designer Viktor Schreckengost, fresh from the classrooms of Vienna, designed and modelled a complete informal set of dinnerware — coupe shaped and glazed in a series of brilliant colors.

Five years elapsed before an interested manufacturer, Charles Sebring of the Sebring Pottery, made a set of molds. Ware from the molds was shown at the New York Metropolitan Museum of Art in the 17th exhibition of contemporary design in February 1935.

Schreckengost's work proved to be the forerunner of today's colorful glaze lines in dinnerware. But his exhibit, glazed in deep gun metal and contrasting oyster white, failed to elicit commercial response in 1935.

Magazines of the day gave Schreckengost's exhibit considerable notice, but so far as the market was concerned, Schreckengost was literally "25 years ahead of time" with his black and white contrast glazes.

This winter — nearly a quarter century since he conceived it — Schreckengost's design has become Salem China Company's newest line of dinnerware, the "Constellation", a contemporary design for casual living.

The "Day and Night" pattern features soft textured off-white art glaze flecked with dark grey-blue, with contrasting pieces in deep charcoal grey which has the soft luster of rich ebony,

Designed to extend the usefulness of the regular dinner set into other fields, the versatile "Constellation" line captures the gay informality of an afternoon party while retaining the dignified charm of formal black and white.

"In our new "Constellation" line we have high style in color contrast which makes the service at home in any setting —formal or informal," J. Harrison Keller, Salem president, said in announcing the new product.

In his fusion of round and square shapes, Schreckengost has achieved exceptional utility. Covered jugs make them suitable for refrigerator storage or outdoor use, [and] help keep contents hot or cold.

A black iron trivet holds the cofee warmer and there's another trivet for the covered server which features a divided vegetable dish insert. The lid of the covered server may be used as a hot pad. Food may be kept warm by pouring hot water around the divided insert in the server.

All pieces are ovenproof. The complete line, including a host of functional pieces and special items, is immediately available from open stock.

Constellation
Shapes

104

Constellation Shapes.
Individual casserole, $45-50;
large covered casserole,
$55-60; divided vegetable,
$40-45

Unidentified shape

Back row: black creamer $20-25, small jug $25-30, large coffee server with lid and with stand $80-85, black jug with lid $45-60, Front row: white gravy, coupe shape cup and saucer $18-20

Ad for Jackstraw Blue from a Crockery & Glass Journal for December 1954

Jackstraw decoration pumpkin colored glaze $14-16

Blue background Jackstraw decoration – Coupe shape used with the Constellation shape, plate $14-16

Southwind decoration on Constellation, also used on other shapes, plate $18-20

Sample dark brown Constellation, not believed to have been produced. No price established

A Comstock decoration designed by Pat Pritchard on Viktor Schreckengost's Free form shape. Courtesy of Craig Barnes

1955 "Free Form" Shape

A flurry of correspondence was exchanged among the Salem sales manager, Jim Armstrong, the patent attorneys, and Harrison Keller concerning the name "Free Form." The Metlox China Company had been using the name "California Freeform" for two years prior to Viktor Schreckengost's designing the "Free Form" shape for Salem. A letter dated June 27, 1956, from the patent attorneys, tells the Salem China Company that their application for the "Free Form" trademark had been approved and passed for publication. The mark was published in the *Official Gazette of the United States Patent Office* on July 17, 1956.

This unusual hollowware had three small feet. The footed cup in "Free Form" was the first cup granted a patent in a hundred years, for its "dripless" feature.

The "Free Form" shape was a departure from the existing traditional shapes. In his own words, designer Viktor Schreckengost described his new "Free Form" dinnerware shape:

The new "Free Form" shape by Salem is [a] contemporary concept of dinnerware design. Each piece expresses its use and function in a pure abstract, sculptural beauty, without the usual restrictions imposed by tradition. As the architect or sculptor builds his compositions from abstract volumes and shapes, so has our designer-sculptor composed each piece as a sculptural expression of beauty and form. Each piece was conceived for its own sake, but one feels a coordinated relationship of character in the entire set. There is not the usual repetition of obvious details to hold the set together, but an overall concept, varying their character and shape as function demands. One motif, which is common to many of the hollowware pieces, is the tripod leg pattern. They are varied in size and proportion, tapering out of the bottom contours to give a light airiness and detachment from the surfaces on which they are placed. One senses the completeness of the forms as they sweep down under and up again to the varying top contours.

To point out specific examples, let us look at the sugar, creamer, and teapot. The globular form of the sugar continues out of the bowl, up into the cover, and terminates in a flowing sweep of the knob-handle. It is a chubby, smooth, little orb, supported on its little tripod tapered legs. The creamer is a taller oval, with a sweeping flourish in its top contour, with soft dimples in the sides, which invite you to pick it up in the right way for pouring. The teapot on the other hand is a low, elongated, gourd-shaped, oval with a long tapering spout and up-swept handle. The lid carries a continuation of the bottom form and terminates in a sprout-like knob. Here we have found quite a variation in the basic form structure as dictated by the duty each is to perform and, at the same time, an intriguing relationship, one to another. The salt and pepper shakers carry on this same "free form" idea, each with its own personality, each becoming part of an overall harmony. The tapering three-leg motif, varies in position and angle, each planned as an integrated part of the piece it is to support.

The cup is a smooth hemisphere, again supported on three tapering legs. These legs support the bowl of the cup free from the saucer, permitting the form and glaze to flow in an uninterrupted line under the bottom. This leg support of the cup influences the saucer, which has a depressed ring into which the legs slide, automatically centering the cup in the saucer. It appears so natural, one wonders why it has not been done before.

The vegetable dishes and decorative serving bowl are variations on the smooth, gourd-like shapes which are wonderful in use. They glamorize the food served in them and immediately suggest for hors d'oeuvres, potato chips, popcorn, nuts, relishes, fruit, and candy, and are wonderful for flower arrangements or as decorative pottery accessories.

The flowing lines, and sweeping top contours, carry on onto the big low fruit bowl and unusual chop-platter. These are the gradual transition to the smooth simplicity of the coup-shaped plates and other place setting pieces. The simplicity of the flatware serves as an excellent foil to accent the hollowware without overdoing the theme.

GLAZE

To accent and show off to the best advantage these unusual forms, a new glaze was developed. It reflects a soft, semi-matt sheen, which highlights the smooth flowing contours. It is opaque white into which has been suspended little flecks of warm, honey-toned color. Due to the depth of suspension within the glaze, the tone value varies, giving a warm, rich appetizing background for food. Their softness of sheen adds an art ware quality. From the utilitarian point of view, the glaze is hard, easily washed, and will not retain germs. It is so formulated that it may be used for baking or refrigerator storage as well as serving.

"FREE FORM" PATTERNS

To add greater variety to the forms, a series of patterns have [sic] been developed which are as unusual and sensible as the dinnerware itself. They vary from the contemporary abstractions to the traditional in subject matter, but none of them are ordinary. Each has been perfectly planned to become a part of the form on which it is used.

HOPSCOTCH: is an intriguing pattern of crossbars of color and textural lines. A variety of these motifs are scattered over the surfaces to prevent monotony or repetition. Each piece has been carefully studied so that just the right amount of decoration appears. Abstract in character.

It has been done in a two-tone pink and charcoal, and a two-tone turquoise blue and charcoal. They are perfect for contemporary interiors.

DAYBREAK: Another overall interest pattern, designed for its interesting distribution of color and texture. Abstract in feeling, but the flowing leaf forms are recognizable. The soft turquoise and charcoal gray suggest the plant forms emerging from the misty cool morning light. Wonderful for both contemporary or provincial.

PRIMITIVE: Inspired by the early cave drawings in southern France, this pattern is first of all good decoration with its warm terra cotta red and sepia brown motifs. The subject matter suggests our earliest records of primitive man as he described and recorded his prowess as a hunter. The little figures and deer romp and play over the set in such a way that one is always surprised and fascinated by their appearance. It would be ideal for many types of settings, and a natural for buffet serving, indoor-outdoor living and ideal for a bachelor setting.

WONDERLAND: A glowing, beautifully imaginative pattern of flowers which suggest the form and shape of many flowers you know but which are really pure fantasy. The variety and sparkle of the overall motifs suggest a wide range of use. It has a quaint charm of the peasant and the suave elegance and sophistication. It is as fresh as a beautiful summer garden after a rain and as soft and lovely as a memory. It will be just right in any setting.

The Free Form shape is one of the most sought-after of Viktor Schreckengost's designs. The Salem China Company described their new Free-Form shape in their sales literature as follows:

Salem's designer, Viktor Schreckengost, has won 45 design awards in his career. His creation of our "Free Form" shape is perhaps his finest achievement to date. The basic forms of "Free Form" are not round, square, or oval; but there is a combination of many pleasing geometric forms; one growing out of the other to become a new form. Handles, knobs, lugs, and spouts flow out of the basic shapes to satisfy the utility and accent the forms. The tripod legs and the globular forms contain freshness and freedom of concept. There is not the usual repetition of obvious details to hold the set together; but an overall smoothness of simplicity, lightness, and arrested motion. Each item is a conversation piece. Free Form has it's own specially created matted glaze; flecked with warm, honey-colored specks of color to lend an appetizing background to the food served on it. Perhaps the most outstanding piece in this very unusual shape is the footed cup; which is the only drip-less cup ever patented.

Of the several different patterns featured on Free Form, most of them have in common the suggestion of motion. Daybreak is a graceful leaf pattern; abstract in feeling; suggesting plant forms emerging from misty morning light. Southwind shows true Autumnal beauty in the charcoal shaded branch tipped by windswept leaves of soft color.

The Primitive decoration on the Free Form shape. This shape and decoration is one of the most sought after Viktor Schreckengost designs. Far left: bowl $20-25, 13" platter $30-35, plate $28-25, Right front: Serving dish $35-40, Center front: cruet set, complete set consists of tray, salt and pepper set, oil and vinegar cruets $125-150

The Sepia Fruit decoration on the Free Form shape. Front far left: cup and saucer set $25-30 set, back row decorative bowl $25-30, teapot $80-100, creamer $20-25, sugar and cover $30-35, center salt and pepper, each $15-20

The Dogwood decoration on the Free Form shape. Left to right, sugar and cover $20-25, creamer $20-25, cup $10-12

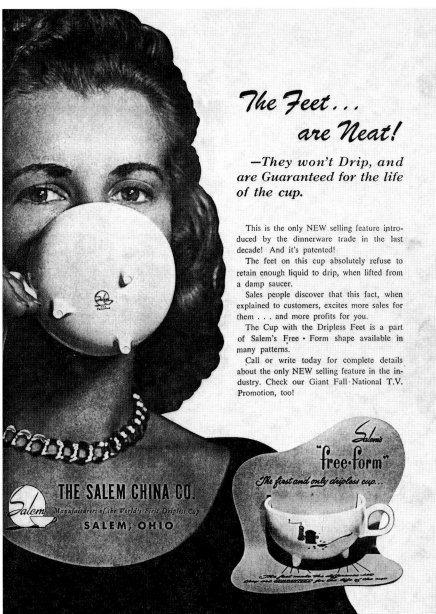

The Feet... are Neat!

—They won't Drip, and are Guaranteed for the life of the cup.

This is the only NEW selling feature introduced by the dinnerware trade in the last decade! And it's patented!

The feet on this cup absolutely refuse to retain enough liquid to drip, when lifted from a damp saucer.

Sales people discover that this fact, when explained to customers, excites more sales for them . . . and more profits for you.

The Cup with the Dripless Feet is a part of Salem's Free • Form shape available in many patterns.

Call or write today for complete details about the only NEW selling feature in the industry. Check our Giant Fall·National T.V. Promotion, too!

THE SALEM CHINA CO.
Manufacturers of the World's First Dripless Cup
SALEM, OHIO

Salem's **"free·form"**
The first and only dripless cup...

Advertisement is from an August 1957 China Glass and Tablewares introducing the new patented dripless cup. The decoration is Down East and is not a Viktor Schreckengost decoration. Other decorations found on the Free Form are Daybreak, Southwind, Hopscotch Pink, Waves, Windblown and Southwind. There may be other decorations.

The Hopscotch Pink decoration on the Free Form shape.

The Southwind decoration on the Free Form shape.

Daybreak

on "free form"*

An over-all interest pattern designed for its interesting distribution of color and texture. Abstract in feeling, but flowing leaf forms are recognizable. Soft turquoise and charcoal gray suggest plant forms emerging from misty-cool morning light. Ideal for both contemporary and provincial interiors.

"free form"

by

Salem

*Name and Shape Copyrighted.

Daybreak decoration on the Free Form shape.

CROCKERY & GLASS JOURNAL for July, 1955   29

Advertisement for the Free Form shape from a July 1955 *Crockery and Glass Journal* showing the first three decorations on Free Form.

Aquaria decoration on Free Form Shape

Waves decoration on the Free Form shape

Windblown decoration on the Free Form shape,

Aquaria round coupe shape plate used with the Free Form shape, plate $15-20

1956 "Contour" Shape

The Contour shape was introduced in 1956. New shapes were discussed in a July, 1956, *China and Glass* article, as follows:

The Salem China Company, Salem, Ohio, has introduced a Shangri-La series on its Contour shape. Whimsical Floral motifs, executed in a sweeping brush line technique, are colorful, and strongly Oriental in flavor.

Patterns include a pale gold chrysanthemum accented by charcoal leaves, done in an unusual arrangement, blue green pine boughs highlighted with delicate pink blossoms fluttering in space, colorful cattails, and delicate fronds of temple moss in grey, chartreuse and moss green.

Suggestive of a quiet afternoon in the Orient is Tea House with dwarf pine and brilliant colored flowers around a tea house, from which pattern derives its name.

A sixteen piece set will retail for $6.95. A 20-piece set for $7.95. Viktor Schreckengost designed and developed the shape and decorations. The Shangri La Series on the Contour shape consisted of Wild Rice, Ming Flower, Teaberry, Blossoms and Pine, Tea House, Swamp Lilly, Marsh Reeds and Temple Moss.

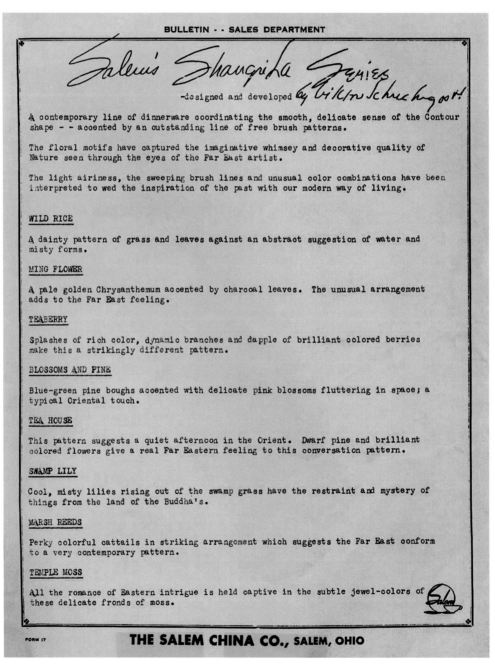

Sales bulletin from the Salem China Company describing eight decorations on the new Contour shape.

April Delicate floral leaves in vertical design enhance the beauty of Salem's "CONTOUR" shape. Notice the unique design of the holloware.

April decoration on the Contour shape. (See miscellaneous section for examples of Contour decorations)

Marsh Reeds coupe shape plate used in the Contour shape, plate $12-14

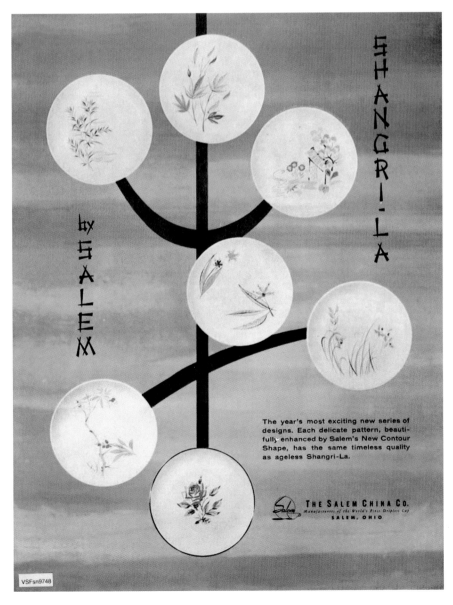

SHANGRI-LA by SALEM

The year's most exciting new series of designs. Each delicate pattern, beautifully enhanced by Salem's New Contour Shape, has the same timeless quality as ageless Shangri-La.

THE SALEM CHINA CO.
Manufacturers of the World's First Dripless Cup
SALEM, OHIO

VSFsn9748

A color ad from the Salem China Company.

The eye-catching holloware of Salem's New Contour Shape is now even more beautiful — with the addition of the ageless beauty of Shangri-La. Here is a series of patterns that has appeal for each customer. Contour Shape is always a display leader — now with the new Shangri-La series of patterns, the imaginative display possibilities will be exceeded only by the acceptance of your customers.

THE SALEM CHINA CO.
Salem, Ohio

VSFsn9798

Black and white ad for Shangri La.

Windblown decoration on the round coupe shape also used on the Free Form shape.

The decoration on this shape may be the Swamp Lily described in the Contour Shangri La section.

1960s "Holiday" Shape

A Holiday shape was mentioned in the Salem correspondence, but no further information has been found.

1961 Cerastone

In 1961, Viktor Schreckengost was asked by Harrison Keller to come up with another name for Ironstone that could apply to their semi-vitreous ware. Keller suggest names like Whitestone, Whetstone, etc. Schreckengost submitted a list of names such as Flintstone, Terrastone, Granite Stone, Dura Stone, Cerastone for the "Vintage Ironstone" ware, and the name Cerastone was accepted.

June 1963 Higbee's department store advertisement showed, at top left: Flyte decoration on Cerastone with Persimmon accessories, top center: Tiki with blue accessories, top far right: Leaf Frolic decoration with olive accessories, center section: Nassau decoration with sandalwood accessories.

Miscellaneous

1934 "Streamline" Shape

The Streamline shape was made by Salem but the design patent belongs to Vincent Broomhall, who worked at the Salem China Company in 1934. Broomhall later became head of design at the Edward M. Knowles pottery company. Streamline was used with Don Schreckengost's Tricorne shape and the already existing Salem Century shape.

1934 "Trend" Shape

The Trend shape, although often attributed to Don Schreckengost, was designed by Vincent Broomhall, who also desgned the Streamline shape for Salem. Broomhall held the patents for both shapes.

1940s Royal Crest True Porcelain

Royal Crest true porcelain ware was designed by Viktor Schreckengost in the 1940s. A beautiful set with wonderful shapes, it consisted of a teapot and a cream and sugar. Royal Crest was never produced and the pottery that made the sample items is thought to be a California pottery company. Royal Crest was glazed in soft pastel colors of blue, yellow, gray, and pink.

Viktor Schuckengost design in true porcelain, not produced. No price established

1960s "North Star" Decoration

For the Salem China Company, the grocery store continuity programs were their "bread and butter." By the 1960s many pottery companies were already out of business, but the Salem China Company managed to stay in business a few more years. The ware used for the continuity programs were a "throwing together" of a few new shapes and a mix of existing shapes and decorations. Sometimes the decorations were given new names. One of the most popular continuity premiums of the Salem China Company was the North Star decoration.

North Star is sought after by collectors and its popularity is more than likely due to the many different items that go with the North Star pattern. The names of the shapes used in North Star have not yet been found. The coupe shape, used in so many of the different Viktor Schreckengost shapes, is the flatware.

Northstar decoration on round coupe shape plate. The Northstar decoration was a large store, continuity premium line that was popular in its time and is highly sought-after by colectors. It has many matching "go-withs.". Northstar plate $12-I4

122

Salem Advertising

A variety of advertising derives from Salem China sales catalogs.

Opposite page, top:
Salem catalog pages showing top row: Blossomtime on the Coronet shape, Woodhue on the Flair shape.
Left center row: Wild Rice on the Contour shape, Simplicity on the round coupe shape Ranchstyle shape, Melody Lane on Ranchstyle, Primrose on the Ranchstyle shape, April on the Contour shape and Hopscotch on the Free Form shape.

Opposite page, bottom:
Salem catalog pages showing (top left) First Lady on the Coronet shape, Anniversary on the Ranchstyle shape, Rural Holiday on the Coronet shape, Jackstraw Accent, Regal Rose (shape not determined).
Bottom row: Melody Lane on the Ranchstyle shape, Woodhue on Flair, Primrose on Ranchstyle, colored glaze ware on the Ranchstyle shape.

Salem China advertisement showing another continuity premium, Pink Bamboo on the same shape as North Star

123

Super market advertisement for Serenade decoration on coupe shape flatware, cup and saucer. Shape of cream and sugar not determined.

Store ad for Bountiful, a wheat decoration. Round coupe shape flatware, cup and saucer. Shape of cream and sugar not determined.

CALICO
Dainty red and gray calico rings encircle a lone, red forget-me-not on Salem's Ranchstyle shape. Pattern is repeated on cups, saucers, sugar, creamer, etc. A red line sets off the edge of the ware.

WOODHUE
An eye-catching array of leaves in "woody" tones of forest brown, spring green, and sky blue on Salem's Flair square coupe shape. A superb table setting for all occasions.

MELODY LANE
An established favorite of modern homemakers. Rose design is dramatized with delicate, yet striking, color effects. Furnished on Salem's modern Ranchstyle coupe shape.

For more than a half century gracious homemakers have preferred fine Salem dinnerware for its price, utility, and pattern selection. Exciting Salem patterns have made dinnerware history all over the country.

Budgetwise homemakers know that when they buy Salem dinnerware they are assured of up-to-the-minute styling and quality. Here's why.

Salem dinnerware is triple selected. Salem dinnerware is triple fired. It must travel through the firing kilns three times, adding more and more strength to it each time.

Salem dinnerware has a lifetime guarantee against crazing. It's ovenproof for utility.

Salem dinnerware is designed by Viktor Schreckengost, famous dinnerware designer and winner of many awards for his achievements in the dinnerware design field.

Remember these outstanding facts about the Salem dinnerware you see on these pages. Any Salem pattern you choose here for your very own is an excellent and wise selection.

BLOSSOMTIME
You can almost smell pink apple blossoms around the edges of the ware. Blossom sprays appear discreetly on cups, sugar, creamer, etc. A most popular pattern on Salem's Coronet shape.

FIRST LADY
Impressively formal. A 23-karat gold design on a rich green background frames the stylized floral design. Footed cups and elegant holloware pieces complete the pattern. Furnished on Salem's famous Coronet shape.

COMPOSITION OF SETS

35-PIECE SET—SERVES 6
1 Platter
1 Vegetable Dish
1 Covered Sugar (2 pcs.)
1 Creamer

53-PIECE SET—SERVES 8
8 Fruit Dishes
1 Large Platter
1 Vegetable Dish
1 Covered Sugar (2 pcs.)
1 Creamer

IMMEDIATE DELIVERY.
F.O.B. OHIO FACTORY

PRIMROSE
Scarlet blooms and buds contrast with rich green leaves in this refreshing pattern on Salem's Ranchstyle shape. Full handles on cups, sugar and creamer add maximum utility value to these items.

COUNTRYSIDE
A variety of farm scenes attractively decorate each of the different items in the set. Excellent for informal entertaining. Durable handles are a feature of this wanted pattern on Salem China's Ranchstyle shape.

SIMPLICITY
Simple in creation, yet delicately intricate and masterfully applied. A lone, sky blue bud appears on a gray-leaved stem. Same motif is repeated five times as the center pattern on the dinnerplates ... once on creamer, sugar, cups, saucers, etc. Made on Salem's Ranchstyle shape.

Salem China color advertisement. Top left: Calico on the Ranchstyle coupe shape. Top right, Blossomtime on the Coronet shape, Middle row: Woodhue on the Flair square coupe shape, Melody Lane on Ranchstyle coupe shape, First Lady on the Coronet shape. Bottom row: Primrose on the Ranchstyle coupe shape. Countryside decoration, coupe shape flatware, and cup and saucer with Flair sugar and creamer. Simplicity decoration on the round coupe Ranchstyle shape.

4 PIECE ASHTRAY SET.................$1.50
REGULAR RETAIL VALUE...$3.75

BEVERAGE SERVER & WARMER...............$1.98
REGULAR RETAIL VALUE...$7.95

13" PLATTER & VEGETABLE BOWL 9".....$1.25
REGULAR RETAIL VALUE...$5.15

TASTEFUL, CHARMING, YET PRACTICAL ...ITS SUPERB QUALITY GUARANTEED ...THAT'S BEAUTIFUL BISCAYNE DINNERWARE. YOU'LL LOVE ITS SMART STYLING, THE SIMPLE GRACE AND FRESHNESS OF ITS MODERN LEAF PATTERN IN TURQUOISE BLUE AND BEIGE WITH TURQUOISE BLUE ACCENT PIECES.

OVENPROOF...
No need to transfer food from one dish to another or move Biscayne out of the refrigerator and let it stand right in the oven! Beautiful Biscayne can take it.

DISHWASHER TOUGH
Ordinary care in handling Biscayne is all that's necessary — Beautiful Biscayne will give you wonderful service for a lifetime.

GUARANTEE...
Beautiful Biscayne is triple fired and triple-selected. It is guaranteed free from crazing for the lifetime of the ware.

1 QT. COVD. BAKING DISH & WARMER.....$1.75
REGULAR RETAIL VALUE...$6.95

Biscayne decoration late 1950s and 1960s. The beverage server is a Viktor Schreckengost design according to company correspondence. The plates are the same round coupe shape used in other lines.

COVERED SUGAR BOWL, CREAMER.......$1.25
REGULAR RETAIL VALUE...$5.20

GRAVY BOAT, SALT & PEPPER SHAKER.....$1.25
REGULAR RETAIL VALUE...$6.35

Left top: Autumn Leaves on the Contour shape. This decoration was called Southwind when used on another shape. Top: Jamaica, Martinique (Hopscotch decoration) Left: Wild Rice on the Contour shape, Simplicity on the Ranchstyle coupe shape, Bottom, Something Blue, Nassau, Castlewood on Coronet shape.

Tulip Time from a Salem advertisement. Plates, saucer and cup are the Ranchstyle round coupe shape. The shape of the creamer and sugar are unknown at this time. Creamer and sugar appears to be a redesign of the Contour or some other shape.

Circle of Flowers, round coupe shape flatware.
Unidentified hollowware shape.

Woodhue decoration on round coupe
shape flatware and cup. Unidentified
creamer and sugar shape.

Royal Joci decoration is a coin gold decoration of wheat spray. The flatware is on the round coupe shape with different shape holloware. I do not believe that the wheat decoration is a Viktor Schreckengost but the shapes are V.S. designs.

Yours~

WITH OUR COMPLIMENTS

GENUINE

ROYAL JOÇI

OVENPROOF DINNERWARE
Hand decorated with 23 car. gold

a FREE gift for YOU!

Newspaper ad for Orchard decoration on the Vintage Ironstone

Unidentified Decorations on Round Coupe Shape

We can give a decoration a name, but if it is not known what hollowware was used with it, it is useless. Decoration names were different when used on different shapes. These coupe shape plates may or may not have been produced, but they are Viktor Schreckengost designs.

Black, gray and golden geometric shapes. The decoration reminds one of paper clips.

Nassau decoration, late 1950s early 1960s, see catalog reprints.

This decoration has been called
Waves or Clouds

This decoration has been called
Pine Branches, probably goes
with Contour.

Bright orange flower with charcoal leaves.

Vivid teal blue flower with charcoal leaves.

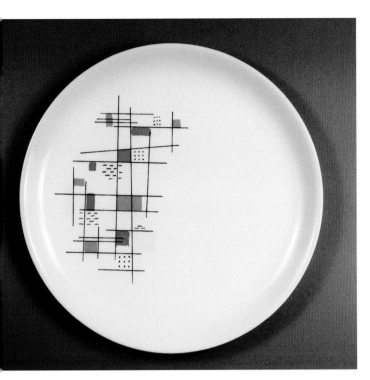

This decoration has been called Mardi Gras

This decoration has been called Fruits and Leaves.

This decoration has been called Grape Leaves.

Jackstraw decoration, but the name may be different on the different colored glazes.

White Daisy like flowers with yellow centers on deep blue background

Large Lily type flower with butterflies

Salem Specialty Items

Salem's specialty items included decorative fancy plates, moustache cups, service plates, children's feeding dishes, ash trays and novelty items. The old Imperial shape was used for service plates and decorative plates. Viktor Schreckengost did not design the shape, but he did design many decorations used on the specialty plates. In this series of plates, Viktor Schreckengost designed the shoulder decoration of flags.

General MacArthur plate, all plates in this series $20-25

Admiral Leahy

Admiral Nemitz

General Eisenhower

Admiral King

General Marshall

Franklin D. Roosevelt

General Arnold

CHARMING
Demitasses
TO CATCH THE SHOPPER'S EYE

Your customers will love these charming demitasses. They're cute, beautifully shaped and have rich, colorful patterns. They're *right* for all gift occasions. Shown above: top left GODEY PRINTS; at right LANSDOWNE; below ARISTOCRAT MAROON. Will retail at 59c to $1.00. Order an assortment of your own choosing, or send for prices and complete information.

THE SALEM CHINA CO.
SALEM, OHIO

Black and white advertising for Demitasses, Jumbo Size cups and saucers, and an ashtray.

The Answer to *"ONE CUP ONLY"*

JUMBO SIZE
Cups and Saucers

You'll get jumbo-size profits by featuring these Jumbo cups and saucers. Double capacity. Sell on sight all year 'round. Suggested retail price —$1.25 to $1.50 each. Sparkling white china with decoration in genuine 23 karat gold. Send trial order, or write for full information and prices.

THE SALEM CHINA CO.
SALEM, OHIO

Commemorative Plates

Another
NEW
Commemorative Plate

Above — The new Cali-
a Plate featuring Yosemite
in center. Around the rim:
Francisco Bay Bridge, Santa
bara Mission, Monterey Cy-
a, Giant Cactus at San Jacinto,
e Capitol, Hollywood Bowl, plus
e Mission Bells.

plates 11" in diameter in soft,
tones of green, brown, and yel-
Watch for other new plates of
is to be added in the future.

A 1949 Crockery and Glass Journal advertise-
ment for "Another NEW Commemorative Plate"
The fifth in the series, the new California plate
pictures Yosemite Falls, San Francisco Bay
Bridge, Santa Barbara Mission, Monterey
Cypress, Giant Cactus at San Jacinto, State
Capitol, Hollywood Bowl, plus three Mission
Bells. All plates 11" in diameter in soft rich tones
of green, brown, and yellow." The first four
commemorative plates were Washington, D.C.,
Boston, Chicago and Philadelphia.

NOW Salem announces a fifth Commemorative
Plate . . . California . . . during the centennial
of this great state. Now you can offer an assortment
of beautiful souvenir plates . . . all collectors' items
. . . all good traffic builders . . . profit makers. Priced
to sell at $2.25 to $2.50 each. Special trial assortment
(your selection) $14.40 per doz. *Order today!*

THE SALEM CHINA CO.

SALEM, OHIO   *Established 1898*

SALES OFFICES: *New York:* H. G. Heckmann, 1107 Broadway,
Chelsea 2-8848 • *Chicago:* Williams & Son, 15-125 Merchandise Mart,
Superior 8922 • *San Francisco:* Leo D. Holtzberg, 274 Western Mer-
chandise Mart, Un. 1-2727 • *Denver, Portland, Seattle:* The Vinton Co.

Sturdi-Ware was a tough, lightweight,
banquet service for churches,
fraternal orders, hospitals, and
institutions on the coupe shape.

THREE PIECE CHILD SETS
ON STURDI-WARE

A new treatment of old favorites! Bo-Peep and the Playful Bears! A combination of pinks, blues, and yellows have made these old favorite subjects into delightful juvenile patterns. Each piece is encircled by a bright 23 karat gold line.

Salem's Sturdi-Ware is used. The rolled edge of the plate and bowl resists edge chips. The reinforcing ridges give strength without adding weight — and the ridges give "sure grip" in washing and handling. Sturdi-Ware is hospital tested and approved. It is cheaper because it will outlast all other ware.

<u>PATTERNS</u>:   Little Bo-Peep   The Playful Bears

Three-piece child's set on Salem's Sturdi-Ware. The Playful Bears consists of 7" plate, mug, cereal bowl, Bo-Peep is made up of the same three pieces.

Original decals for the Hobby Horse line

8 In. Compt. Feeding Dish

SALEM'S POPULAR JUVENILE DINNERWARE

Mother Goose Subjects, No. 70106

THE SALEM CHINA CO.
SALEM, OHIO

Hobby Horse Series, No. 70141 GE

8 In. Compt. Feeding Dish

Hobby Horse Series and
the Mother Goose Series

Hobby Horse series plate,
bowl, and mug

Original decal for the Hobby Horse line

Three-compartment Alphabet child's feeding dish with Hobby Horse decoration

Mother Goose subjects

Bibliography

Section One, American Limoges China Company

Adams, Henry. *Viktor Schreckengost and 20th Century Design*. Cleveland: The Cleveland Museum of Art, 2005.

Bagdade, Susan & Al. *Warman's American Pottery and Porcelain.* Radnor, Pa.: Wallace-Homestead Cook Co., 1994, p. 201-203.

Blaszczyk, Regina Lee. *Imagining Consumers: Design and Innovation from Wedgwood to Corning.* Baltimore: Johns Hopkins University Press, 2000, p. 254-255.

Cunningham Jo. *Collector's Encyclopedia of American Dinnerware: Identification and Values.* 2nd ed. Paducah, Kentucky: Collector Books, 2005, p. 210.

Duke, Harvey. *Official Price Guide to Pottery and Porcelain.* 8th ed. New York: House of Collectibles, 1995, p. 447-453.

Gates, William C., Jr., & Dana E. Ormerod. *The East Liverpool, Ohio, Pottery District: Identification of Manufacturers and Marks.* [Rockville, MD]: Society for Historical Archaeology, 1992, p. 170-183.

Lehner, Lois. *Lehner's Encyclopedia of U.S. Marks on Pottery, Porcelain & Clay.* Paducah, Ky.: Collector Books, c1988, p. 262-264.

McKee, Floyd W. *The Second Oldest Profession: A Century of American Dinnerware Manufacture.* [S.l.]: The Author, 1966, p. 40-41, and 45.

Nelson, Linda. *O, Beautiful American Limoges.* http://www.suite101.com/article.cfm/american_dinnerware/70625. June 1, 2001.

Ohio Industrial Biography, 18. The Limoges China Company. The Ohio State University Engineering Experiment Station News, Oct. 1946), p. 8-10.

Woodard, Kathy L. *Profiles in Ceramics: Viktor Schreckengost. The American Ceramic Society Bulletin,* vol. 80, no. 1 (Jan. 2001), p. 40-46.

Section Two, Salem China Company

Adams, Henry. *Viktor Schreckengost and 20th Century Design*. Cleveland: The Cleveland Museum of Art, 2005.

Bagdade, Susan & Al. *Warman's American Pottery and Porcelain.* Radnor, Pa.: Wallace-Homestead Cook Co., 1994, p. 138-139.

Blaszczyk, Regina Lee. *Imagining Consumers: Design and Innovation from Wedgwood to Corning.* Baltimore: Johns Hopkins University Press, 2000, p. 151-153, and 254-255.

Cunningham Jo. *Collector's Encyclopedia of American Dinnerware: Identification and Values.* 2nd ed. Paducah, Kentucky: Collector Books, 2005, p. 246-255.

_____. *Best of Collectible Dinnerware*, 2nd ed. Atglen, Pennsylvania: Schiffer Publishing, 1999.

Duke, Harvey. *Official Price Guide to Pottery and Porcelain.* 8th ed. New York: House of Collectibles, 1995, p.667-682.

Gates, William C., Jr., & Dana E. Ormerod. *The East Liverpool, Ohio, Pottery District: Identification of Manufacturers and Marks.* [Rockville, MD]: Society for Historical Archaeology, 1992, p. 247.

Lehner, Lois. *Lehner's Encyclopedia of U.S. Marks on Pottery, Porcelain & Clay.* Paducah, Ky.: Collector Books, c1988, p. 396-401.

McKee, Floyd W. *The Second Oldest Profession: A Century of American Dinnerware Manufacture.* [S.l.]: The Author, 1966, p. 44-45.

Pratt, Michael E. *Salem China Company.* http://www.modish.net/salem_china.php, 2004.

Woodard, Kathy L. Profiles in Ceramics: Viktor Schreckengost. The American Ceramic Society bulletin, vol. 80, no.1 (Jan. 2001), p. 40-46.

Index